The Great British Farmhouse Cookbook

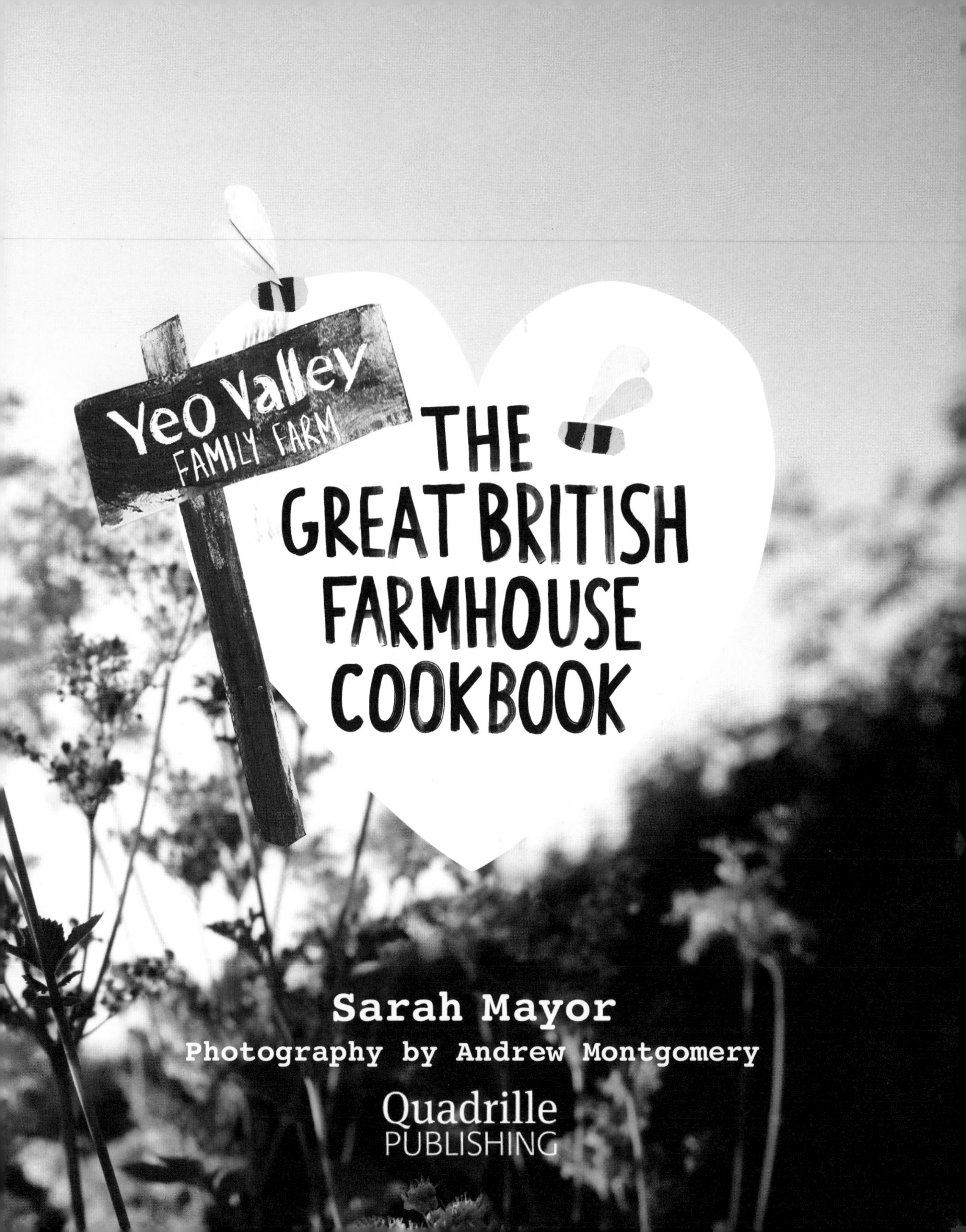

Yeo Valley
FAMILY FARM

THE GREAT BRITISH FARMHOUSE COOKBOOK

Sarah Mayor

Photography by Andrew Montgomery

Quadrille
PUBLISHING

Contents

........6
Introduction....................8
From pasture to pot 10
The Dairy 46
The Farmhouse Kitchen.........74
The Veg Garden.....................104
The Farmyard 130
The Pastures........................156
The Woods, Hedgerows,
Fields & Streams 188
The Fruit Garden................218
Recipe list 220
Index 224
Acknowledgements ....

The cookbook in your hands is one very much rooted in a place. That place is the Yeo Valley, a beautiful part of Somerset, which lies between the Mendip Hills and the Chew Valley, and is where I grew up and live today. Dad's family have been farming here in the West Country since the days of the 15th century and he and Mum bought our farm on the edge of Blagdon Lake in 1961.

Food has always been a huge part of my life. Well, when you're surrounded by such amazing produce — fruit, vegetables, fish, wonderful meat and dairy — it's hard to not to be inspired to cook. And so from a young age, if I wasn't helping to look after the calves, or dangling worms into the pond in hope of trout, I'd be busy in the kitchen helping Mum.

This makes it all sound rather idyllic. Well in some ways I suppose it was. But it was also ruddy hard work. From a young age it was all hands on deck, for me and for my brother Tim and sister Amanda. We'd help with everything: feeding the cows, lambing, calving, not to mention the enviable task of mucking out. Always a favourite!

At the time, and this would have been the mid-Sixties, we had all sorts of animals: cows, sheep, ponies, chickens, turkeys. A few years after that, we started growing potatoes, sweetcorn and strawberries, and started a 'pick your own' business. Visitors were always saying how they loved our picturesque spot in the valley by the lake, so we decided to set up a tea room serving scones and jam and lovely clotted cream made from our own milk. Soon we had queues stretching right up to the main road!

But making lots of clotted cream left us with a problem: what to do with all the skimmed milk we had left over. Then Dad had the genius idea of making yogurt. I say 'genius idea'. Actually, at the time, it seemed a bit bonkers. You have to remember that these were days before you could pick up things like lemongrass and pomegranates from your local supermarket.

These were days before supermarkets full stop. Put it this way: at the time, olive oil was considered exotic. Our first yogurt contract wasn't even with a shop; it was with a Bristol hospital!

Thankfully, Dad's energy, drive and foresight paid off. There was a massive food revolution in this country and people started to realise that yogurt wasn't just good for you — it was delicious, too. Gradually it became the centre of the family farm, and we haven't looked back since.

It wasn't just Dad who was being inspired by this revolution in food; I was, too. By this time, I was a fully fledged, card-carrying foodie. I had learned so much from my life on the farm, but I was hungry for more. So in 1979, I traded my beloved West Country for London and a career in catering, though it wasn't long before I was lured back to Somerset, where I settled down to have my three children. When the youngest had reached school age, a friend of mine asked me if I might want to teach at her cookery school, The Grange. I'd never taught before, so I was a little, how shall we say, hesitant? Well, she twisted my arm, and I'm really glad she did. The students were fantastic and I thoroughly enjoyed sharing my skills and encouraging them to use their senses: to smell, to touch, to taste. To think about seasonality, about where their food comes from and, in the case of meat, how the animal has been raised. It was also great for me to be able to share my love of the social side of food, the joy — and importance — of sitting around with family and friends to share a wonderful meal.

It's funny, lots of things don't seem to have
changed that much over the years. Yes, the farm
is much bigger these days, but the same things that
were important then are important now. As a family,
we still all live within about six miles of each
other. My brother Tim, who runs Yeo Valley,
lives in the house we grew up in. Mum lives in
a village just down the road. I'm a stone's throw
away on my own organic farm and my sister, Amanda,
is just a short drive from us. We're all still
very involved in Yeo Valley, just as we always
have been. And good food, made with local, seasonal
ingredients, is as important to us as it ever was.

We now have a fantastic restaurant at our HQ, which
is open to the people who work for Yeo Valley and
anyone who comes to use our spaces for conferences
and that sort of thing. For me to have had the
opportunity to bring everything I learned in my
cooking career back to the farm has been incredibly
satisfying, and not something I ever imagined would
happen. I've very much enjoyed planning a whole
year's worth of seasonal menus for our kitchens,
all of which make full use of the lovely organic
produce from our gardens, farm and dairy.

On the following pages are some of my absolute
favourite recipes, all of them inspired by my
surroundings and my journey as a cook. I'd describe
them as classic British farmhouse dishes with
a modern twist. Some are things we cook in our
restaurant and our tea rooms; others are based
on meals we enjoyed as children. The rest are
dishes we like to eat at home when spending time
with family and friends. We're a big family —
9 grandchildren at the last count — and this
is family food; food to eat together. I've had
a fantastic year of cooking, tasting and tweaking.
I very much hope you enjoy the results.

From pasture to pot

Somerset has a fantastic climate for growing grass. So, if you're a farmer who lives here, the sensible thing to do is to keep dairy cows. All ours are British Friesians: they're a hardy breed that thrives on lush pastures.

Our Lakemead pedigree herd, which is 400-strong, is divided across two farms. One is here at Holt Farm, on the edge of Blagdon Lake in the Yeo Valley; the other is at Yoxter Farm, four miles away up on the Mendips.

We make it in pretty much the same way. We add a type of good bacteria to warm milk, the bacteria eat the lactose and this makes lactic acid, which protects the milk from harmful bacteria. It's a little bit like the pickling process. Fancy making yogurt yourself? Turn to page 14 for an easy recipe.

Yogurt was invented as a way to preserve milk, which goes off quickly in warm climates. People found that by adding special bacteria, they could help milk keep for much longer. Ingenious!

Our cows graze on clover-rich grass in the warmer months and then, when it gets a bit cooler, we bring them inside. They have well-ventilated, spacious housing with comfy bedding and plenty of organic winter feed known as silage — a type of pickled grass. We also give them cereals like wheat, barley and triticale. Eating a balanced diet isn't just important for humans!

We have a special and rather large barn, where we rear our calves — up to 400 a year. There's a huge demand for the best of our male calves, which are sold for breeding all over the world. The rest we rear for beef. All the females go back into our milking herd.

Our cows amble into the dairy twice a day for milking, where they each give around 25 litres per day. It takes us three hours to milk 200 cows. And the milk doesn't have far to travel; the place where we make our yogurt is just half a mile away.

We have nine staff looking after the cows, as well as a conservation team, who spend their days dry stone walling, planting trees and keeping the hedges in order. They also look after the Miscanthus, a special type of grass that we use to fuel the biomass boiler, which heats our HQ.

the dairy

Now, this probably won't come as a huge surprise, but we think milk's magical stuff. One little fact we like to recount is that baby blue whales can live for up to five years on their mother's milk alone – it really is packed with goodness. And so versatile! Some good creamy yogurt with granola for breakfast; a blob of crème fraîche stirred through ribbons of fresh pasta for lunch; a knob of fennel and chilli butter on a nice, rare steak for supper. Glorious.

Mum and Margot get ready for the cameras

Our parents set up the farm back in the Sixties, and cows have been part of the family ever since.

Felicity

BRITISH FRIESIAN

We're huge fans of the British Friesian cow, a sturdy breed that thrives on our clover-rich grass.

In the winter, our cows live indoors in the warm where they eat a balanced diet of silage (pickled grass) and grains.

We give each cow their own special mix, depending on which nutrients they need. Talk about individual treatment!

They even have special robotic scrapey things in their quarters which keep things tidy. A nice, clean floor helps make sure their feet stay dry and healthy.

Yogurt

This won't be as thick as shop-bought yogurt but if you want it a little thicker, simply tip it into a muslin-lined sieve and leave it to drain in the fridge for an hour or two until it's a consistency that you like.

Put 1 litre whole milk into a pan and heat it to 85°C. It will be steaming and bubbles will appear around the edge of the pan. Pour it into a very clean bowl and leave it to cool to 43-46°C, then whisk in 65g bio-live natural yogurt. You now need to keep the mixture warm and undisturbed for a minimum of 7-12 hours to thicken (we like to either pour ours into a thermos flask or wrap it in a clean towel and leave it somewhere warm like the airing cupboard, near the Aga or by a radiator). Stir the yogurt well and pour into suitable fridge-sized pots with lids. Chill overnight in the fridge, during which time the yogurt will thicken even more.

MAKES 1 LITRE

Yogurt cheese

This is similar to fresh cream cheese and is made simply by draining natural yogurt overnight to rid it of all its liquid. Rolled into balls and preserved in oil with herbs and other flavourings, these are lovely served with crackers, and maybe a dab of tapenade, basil pesto or sun-dried tomato pesto. They'll keep for a good week in the fridge.

Mix 1.5kg Greek-style natural yogurt with 2 tsp salt. Spoon it into a large sieve lined with a large square of double-thick muslin. Tie the opposite corners of the muslin together, suspend it over the bowl and leave it to drain in the fridge until it stops dripping — about 48 hours. Remove the yogurt cheese from the muslin and discard the whey. Roll the cheese into about 35 x 25g golf-sized balls, and pop them into a sterilised preserving jar with either some fresh herbs, peeled garlic cloves, strips of pared lemon zest, cracked black peppercorns, crushed or whole dried chillies, or a combination of whichever you fancy. Pour extra-virgin olive oil over the cheese to cover, and seal. Leave for 24 hours before serving.

MAKES APPROX. 900G (35 BALLS)

Why not try...?

Using your yogurt to make a spicy feta and roasted red pepper dip

Preheat the oven to 220°C/Gas 7. Rub a red pepper and a chilli with a little olive oil, put them in a small roasting tin and roast for 25 minutes until their skins have blackened. Remove from the oven, seal in a plastic bag and leave to cool, then remove the skin, seeds and stalks, reserving the flesh. Pop into a food processor with 200g feta cheese, 4-5 tbsp Greek-style yogurt and 1 tbsp extra-virgin olive oil and blend into a coarse paste.

Or how about...?

Instead of preserving the cheese in oil, try serving it as a dip sprinkled with herbs and olive oil or a North African spice blend called Za'atar, a mixture of toasted sesame seeds, a thyme-like herb, sumac, and salt.

Ricotta

You can make ricotta using liquid rennet, distilled vinegar, white wine vinegar and even yogurt, but we think this recipe – which uses lemon juice – gives the right combination of taste and consistency. The longer you leave the ricotta to drain the firmer it will become. After 8 minutes the curds are soft and can be eaten just as they are. After 20 minutes they'll have become firm enough to hold their shape but will still be soft. From between 40 and 60 minutes they will be solid enough to cook with. Whatever you do, be sure to use the freshest milk you can lay your hands on – you'll taste the difference.

Line a large sieve with a layer of damp fine muslin. Put 2.25 litres whole milk, in a pan with 250ml double cream and ½ tsp salt, place over a medium-low heat and heat slowly to 93°C, stirring gently occasionally. When it reaches the right temperature the milk will be steaming, the surface will be shimmering and small bubbles will have appeared on the surface. Whip the pan off the heat and stir in 4 tbsp freshly squeezed lemon juice for a few seconds until curds start to form. Leave undisturbed for 2 minutes then, using a slotted spoon, gently ladle the curds into the sieve, taking care not to break them up. Drain until the ricotta reaches the desired consistency (see left). Cover and refrigerate for up to 2 days.

MAKES APPROX. 600G

Why not try...? Baked ricotta with thyme

Preheat the oven to 180°C/Gas 4. Line 4-6 new 8-9cm terracotta flowerpots with baking paper. Mix 350g fresh ricotta with 3 medium free-range egg yolks, 1 tbsp chopped thyme leaves, finely grated zest of 1 small lemon, 25g finely grated parmesan and season to taste. Whisk 3 egg whites into soft peaks and gently fold in. Spoon the lot into the pots and bake for 20-25 minutes until puffed up and golden. Serve warm with toasted bread.

Butter

This butter is deliciously sweet and so much nicer than most of the butter you can find in the shops. The leftover buttermilk isn't quite the same as the cultured stuff that you can buy, but it's still great for making bread.

Put 600ml double cream and ¼ tsp salt (if you like your butter salted) into a food processor and blend until it thickens and separates into butter and buttermilk. Add 4–5 tbsp ice-cold water and continue to process until the butter starts to form into small lumps. Tip the mixture into a sieve set over a bowl to save the buttermilk. This can be chilled for up to 2 days. Put the butter onto a plate and press it with the back of a fork to squeeze out all the excess buttermilk. Gradually it will come together into a ball with no signs of any liquid seeping out. Shape into blocks or balls or press into small pots, cover and chill until needed. This will keep in the fridge for up to 5 days.

MAKES APPROX. 280G

Or how about...?

Flavoured butter. Mix 100g of the soft butter with ¼ tsp salt, some freshly ground black pepper and your choice of flavouring (see below). Spoon the butter onto a sheet of clingfilm, greaseproof paper or non-stick baking paper and shape into a 3cm-wide roll. Wrap up tightly and chill until firm.

1. Fennel seed, chilli & garlic – 1 tsp crushed fennel seeds, ½ finely chopped chilli, ¼ tsp crushed dried chillies and 2 crushed garlic cloves. 2. Blue cheese – 50g rich buttery blue cheese and 1 tsp chopped thyme leaves. 3. Sun-dried tomato, rosemary & olive – 15g each of finely chopped sun-dried tomatoes and pitted black olives, 1 small crushed garlic clove, and 1 tsp finely chopped rosemary. 4. Tarragon & garlic – 2 tbsp chopped tarragon and 2 crushed garlic cloves.

Cream cheese

To make a firmer cheese that you can slice, wrap the curds tightly in the muslin and refrigerate overnight.

Put 1 litre whole milk into a pan and warm it gently until it reaches 37°C. Pour into a bowl, stir in 5 tsp rennet and leave somewhere cool (but not in the fridge) for 2 hours or until set. Then break up the curds with a fork and stir in 3/4 tsp salt. Line a large sieve with a double sheet of muslin, rest it over a bowl and pour in the cheesy curds. Cover and leave somewhere cool (but again, not the fridge) overnight.

MAKES APPROX. 200G

Why not try...?
Cream cheese hearts with vanilla sugar

Line 6 heart-shaped coeur à la crème moulds with damp muslin and place on a rack over a small roasting tin. Press 200g cream cheese through a sieve into a mixing bowl. Lightly whip 225ml double cream with 25g caster sugar until it just starts to form soft peaks then gently fold it into the cream cheese. Spoon into the prepared moulds, cover and chill for 2 hours. Turn out onto small plates and serve sprinkled with a little vanilla sugar (either pre-bought or made by mixing the seeds from 1 vanilla pod into 50g sifted caster sugar) and some chilled pouring cream.

Crème fraîche

Homemade crème fraîche has a wonderful texture and flavour. If you find yourself wanting to make a second lot, reserve a few tablespoons from the first batch and use that instead of the buttermilk. The results will be thicker and even more delicious.

Pour 200ml double cream into a small mixing bowl and stir in 2 tbsp cultured buttermilk. Cover with clingfilm and leave in a warm room for 24 hours. After that, the mixture should have thickened and taken on a pleasant sour flavour. Cover and chill until needed, during which time it will thicken to the perfect texture. It will keep in the fridge for up to 1 week.

MAKES APPROX. 250G

Now try...

Tagliatelle with crème fraîche, butter & cheese

Mix 250g crème fraîche with 4 medium free-range egg yolks, 75g finely grated parmesan and some salt and pepper. Toss together with 500g cooked, drained egg tagliatelle and 30g unsalted butter over a low heat for 1 minute until the sauce has lightly thickened, then serve with a bit of extra grated parmesan.

Clotted cream

This homemade clotted cream is delicious with scones or puds and will keep for up to 5 days in the fridge.

Preheat the oven to 80°C. Pour 600ml double cream into a 28 x 18cm shallow ceramic baking dish and cover tightly with foil, then bake the cream for 10-12 hours or overnight until the top forms a thick, pale-yellow crust and the rest of the cream underneath has reduced and thickened slightly. Remove from the oven and leave to cool, then cover with clingfilm and chill in the fridge for 8 hours or overnight. To use, scoop off the thick cream on top (this is the clotted cream). The remaining thinner cream can be used in ordinary cooking.

MAKES APPROX. 300G

Now why not try...?
Clotted cream ice-cream Put 600ml whole milk and 225g clotted cream into a non-stick pan. Scrape out the seeds from 1 vanilla pod, add the pod and seeds to the pan and bring to the boil. Set aside for 20 minutes to infuse. Whisk 6 medium egg yolks and 175g caster sugar together in a bowl until pale and thick. Return the milk to the boil, then remove the vanilla pod and stir the lot into the egg yolks. Strain into the cleaned-out pan and cook over a gentle heat, stirring constantly, until the mix has thickened and lightly coats the back of a wooden spoon. Pour back into the bowl and leave to cool, then cover and chill overnight. The next day churn the mixture in an ice-cream maker. Spoon into a plastic container, cover and freeze until needed.

Milk shakes

The thing to bear in mind here is that the creamier the milk and the other ingredients, the richer and more unctuous the shake will be. We make ours with Greek-style or wholemilk yogurt or, if we really want to push the boat out, a good ice-cream. Here are four of our favourite combinations. All you need to do is blitz the ingredients together with a few ice cubes.

Strawberry – 250ml ice-cold whole milk, 100g vanilla ice-cream or full-fat natural or strawberry yogurt, 250g ripe de-hulled berries and 1 tbsp honey if needed.

Chocolate – 250ml ice-cold whole milk, 100g vanilla ice-cream or full-fat natural yogurt, 25g optional piece of homemade honeycomb (see page 63) and 100g chocolate spread or chocolate and nut spread.

Banana – 250ml ice-cold whole milk, 100g ripe peeled banana, 100g vanilla ice-cream or full-fat natural yogurt, 1 tbsp maple syrup if needed and 1 tsp vanilla bean paste or extract.

Peanut butter – 250ml ice-cold whole milk, 100g vanilla ice-cream or full-fat natural yogurt, 100g smooth organic peanut butter with no added sugar and 1 tbsp honey or agave syrup if needed.

MAKES 1 REALLY LARGE GLASS (or a bottle)

It's recipes like this that make us rejoice in finding a few spare lumps of stilton at the back of the fridge. Within a few minutes you can have a rich and creamy soup on the table. If you're not in the mood for making the scones, crusty bread never disappoints.

Celery & stilton soup with hot potato scones

SERVES 4–6

40g butter

1 large onion, chopped

300g celery stalks, thinly sliced

15g plain flour

750ml good chicken stock

125g de-rinded creamy blue cheese, such as Colston Bassett stilton, crumbled

80ml single cream

chopped chives to garnish

salt and freshly ground black pepper

FOR THE POTATO SCONES:

100g floury potatoes, peeled and cut into chunks

175g plain flour, plus extra for rolling out

1 tbsp baking powder

50g chilled butter, cut into pieces

60ml whole milk

1. Melt the butter in a large pan, add the onion and celery, cover and cook over a low heat for 20 minutes until really soft but not coloured. Stir in the flour and cook gently for 1 minute, then gradually stir in the stock and bring to the boil. Cover and leave to simmer for 20 minutes.

2. Meanwhile, make the scones. Preheat the oven to 220°C/Gas 7. Tip the potatoes into a pan of well-salted water, bring to the boil and simmer for 15 minutes or until tender. Drain and leave for the steam to die down, then mash and leave to cool.

3. Sift the flour, baking powder and a large pinch of salt into a food processor, add the butter and whiz until it resembles breadcrumbs. Add the potatoes and whiz together briefly, then tip into a mixing bowl and stir in the milk to form a soft dough. Turn the dough out onto a floured surface and knead very lightly into a ball, then roll out to a thickness of 2cm and cut into 6cm rounds, re-kneading and rolling out the trimmings to make 6 small scones. Pop them, slightly apart, on a lightly floured baking tray and bake for about 10 minutes until risen and golden brown.

4. Leave the soup to cool for a few minutes, then liquidise in batches until smooth. Sieve the soup, pour about 500ml into the liquidiser, add the cheese and liquidise until smooth again. Stir back into the remaining soup with the cream and some seasoning and reheat gently. Ladle into warmed bowls, garnish with chopped chives and serve with the hot buttered scones.

You can make this recipe with store-bought ricotta and it will be great. But, if you do like the idea of making your own, your efforts won't go unnoticed. The results will be fabulous. Our recipe for it is on page 16.

Swiss chard, ricotta & lemon cannelloni

SERVES 6

FOR THE TOMATO SAUCE:

1 small onion, quartered

1 small carrot,
cut into rough chunks

1 celery stalk,
cut into rough chunks

1½ tbsp olive oil

600g canned chopped tomatoes

3 fresh bay leaves

1 tsp clear honey

salt and freshly
ground black pepper

FOR THE FILLING:

25g butter

1kg Swiss chard, stalks discarded
and leaves finely shredded

2 garlic cloves, crushed

250g ricotta (see page 16),
well drained

finely grated zest of
1 large lemon

50g parmesan, finely grated

12 sheets (about 300g)
dried lasagne pasta

1 tbsp olive oil

FOR THE CHEESE SAUCE:

600ml whole milk

65g butter

50g plain flour

3 tbsp double cream

150g cheddar, coarsely grated

1 free-range egg yolk

1. For the tomato sauce, put the onion, carrot and celery into a food processor and pulse until finely chopped. Heat the oil in a large pan, add the chopped veg and ¼ teaspoon of salt, then cover and cook over a low heat for 10 minutes, until the veg are soft but not browned. Uncover, add the tomatoes, bay leaves, honey and 100ml water and bring to the boil, stirring. Simmer for about 1 hour, stirring frequently, or until the sauce is reduced and concentrated. Remove the bay leaves, season to taste and leave to cool.

2. For the filling, heat a knob of the butter in a pan, then add as much of the chard as you can. Let it wilt down, then add the rest. Cover and cook for 2-3 minutes, until tender, then tip into a colander and squeeze out as much liquid as possible. Melt the remaining butter in the pan, add the garlic and as soon as it starts sizzling, add the chard leaves and stir to mix. Transfer to a bowl and leave to cool, then stir in the ricotta, zest and parmesan and season to taste.

3. Bring a large pan of salted water to the boil. Spoon the tomato sauce over the base of a large baking dish. Drop the lasagne sheets one at a time into the boiling water, add the oil and cook for 12 minutes or until al dente. Drain well, separate and lay out side by side on a sheet of clingfilm. Divide the chard filling between them, spooning it along one short edge of each sheet. Roll them up and place them side by side, seam-side down on top of the tomato sauce.

4. Preheat the oven to 190°C/Gas 5. Bring the milk to the boil. Melt the butter in another pan, add the flour and gently cook for 1 minute, then beat in the milk and simmer for 10 minutes. Set aside, stir in the cream, half the cheese and egg yolk and some seasoning.

5. Pour the cheese sauce over the top of the cannelloni and sprinkle over the rest of the cheese. Bake for 30-35 minutes or until golden and bubbling.

Soufflé recipes are sometimes rather scary. You never quite know whether they're going to rise triumphantly or sink like a stone. Well, no such worries here.

For a change try…
Serving these soufflés with a salad of sliced tomatoes and chopped fresh herbs like basil, some good olive oil, sea salt and pepper. Just the thing for a summer's day…

Twice-baked goats' cheese soufflés with radish & watercress salad

SERVES 6

300ml whole milk

1 shallot, sliced

2 bay leaves

6 black peppercorns

45g butter, plus extra for greasing

65g parmesan, finely grated

40g plain flour

¼ tsp cayenne pepper

3 medium free-range eggs, separated

100g soft rindless goats' cheese, crumbled

200ml double cream

salt and freshly ground black pepper

FOR THE SALAD:

½ tsp Dijon mustard

1½ tsp red wine vinegar

2½ tbsp extra-virgin olive oil

150g mixed watercress sprigs, pea shoots, lamb's lettuce and baby beet leaves

1 large bunch radishes, topped, tailed and sliced

1. Bring the milk, shallot, bay leaves and peppercorns to the boil in a pan. Set aside for 20-30 minutes to infuse, then strain, discarding the flavourings.

2. Meanwhile, grease 6 x 120ml ramekins with butter and coat the insides with 20g of the parmesan.

3. Preheat the oven to 180°C/Gas 4. Melt the butter in a non-stick pan, add the flour and cook gently over a low heat for 1 minute. Gradually beat in the milk and bring to the boil, stirring. The mixture will be quite thick. Stir in the cayenne pepper, egg yolks, goats' cheese, ½ teaspoon of salt and some pepper, pour into a large mixing bowl and leave to cool slightly.

4. Whisk the egg whites in a clean bowl into soft peaks. Gently fold them into the sauce. Spoon the mix into the ramekins, pop them into a small roasting tin and pour enough boiling water into the tin to come halfway up their sides. Bake for 16-18 minutes, until the soufflés are puffed up and set. Remove the ramekins from the water and leave the soufflés to sink and cool.

5. To serve, heat the oven to 220°C/Gas 7. Carefully turn the soufflés out of the ramekins and arrange them upside-down in a large, lightly buttered baking dish. Season the cream to taste and pour over the soufflés, then sprinkle over the remaining grated parmesan and bake for about 12 minutes until the soufflés have puffed up again and the sauce is golden and bubbling.

6. For the salad, whisk the mustard and vinegar together in a small bowl, then gradually whisk in the oil and season to taste. Toss the dressing through the leaves and radishes and serve with the hot soufflés.

The thing that really sets this tart apart is the pastry, which has a spot of cheddar in it, as well as some oatmeal for a pleasingly nutty bite. As for the filling, any good British blue will do, but we quite like Dorset Blue Vinny.

Blue cheese & leek tart in cheesy oatmeal pastry

SERVES 6-8

FOR THE CHEESY OATMEAL PASTRY:

175g plain flour

65g medium oatmeal

pinch salt

50g chilled butter, cut into small pieces

50g chilled lard, cut into small pieces

75g cheddar, finely grated

FOR THE FILLING:

65g butter

400g trimmed leeks, halved lengthways, cleanedand thinly sliced

300ml whipping or double cream

3 large free-range eggs

150g de-rinded blue cheese, finely crumbled

1 tbsp chopped fresh thyme leaves

salt and freshly ground black pepper

1. For the pastry, pop the flour into a food processor with the oatmeal, salt, butter and lard and whiz briefly until the mixture looks like fine breadcrumbs. Add the grated cheese and whiz again, then stir in 2 tablespoons of ice-cold water and process very briefly until the mixture comes together in a ball.

2. Thinly roll out the pastry and use to line a 25cm loose-bottomed flan tin. Prick the base all over with a fork and chill for 20 minutes. Preheat the oven to 200°C/Gas 6.

3. Line the chilled pastry case with greaseproof paper and a thin layer of baking beans and bake for 15-20 minutes, until the edges of the pastry are biscuit coloured. Remove the paper and beans and return the tin to the oven for 7-8 minutes until the pastry base is golden brown. Remove and set to one side. Reduce the oven temperature to 190°C/Gas 5.

4. For the filling, melt the butter in a large saucepan, add the sliced leeks and season lightly. Cover and cook gently for a couple of minutes until just softened, then uncover and cook for a further 3-5 minutes until the leeks are tender and any excess liquid has evaporated. Leave to cool slightly.

5. Mix the cream and eggs together in a bowl with some salt and pepper to taste. Stir in the leeks, blue cheese and thyme, then pour the mixture into the tart case. Cook in the oven for about 30 minutes until just set and lightly browned on top. Leave to cool slightly before turning out and serving.

Our farm runs alongside Blagdon Lake, which, as well as being beautiful to look at, is absolutely teeming with trout. No surprise then that trout dishes feature rather heavily at home and at our tea rooms.

Deep trout fish cakes with lemon butter & chive sauce

SERVES 4

3 x 300g trout

50g butter, melted

4 spring onions, trimmed and thinly sliced

450g floury potatoes, peeled, cut into chunks and boiled until tender

10g curly leaf parsley, finely chopped

plain flour, for dusting

2 tbsp sunflower oil

salt and freshly ground black pepper

FOR THE LEMON BUTTER SAUCE:

2 tbsp dry white wine

1 tbsp lemon juice

1 small shallot, finely chopped

1 tbsp double cream

75g chilled unsalted butter, cut into tiny pieces

1 tbsp finely chopped chives

1. Preheat the oven to 200°C/Gas 6. Brush the trout with half the melted butter and season well. Pop them on a buttered baking tray and roast for 12–15 minutes, until just cooked through. Leave to cool, then peel back the top layer of skin from each fish and run a knife between the 2 fillets. Carefully ease the fish away from the bones, and flake into small chunky pieces. Leave to drain on kitchen paper.

2. Warm the remaining melted butter in a small pan. Add the spring onions and cook gently for 1 minute. Set to one side. Pop the boiled potatoes into a bowl and mash until smooth, then stir in the spring onions, flaked fish and parsley. Season to taste. Using lightly floured hands, shape the mix into four 5cm-thick fish cakes. Cover and chill for at least 1 hour.

3. To cook the fish cakes, heat the oil in a large frying pan and preheat the oven to 200°C/Gas 6. Dust each cake with more flour, add to the pan and cook over a medium heat for 3-4 minutes on each side until golden brown. Transfer to a greased baking tray and bake for 12-15 minutes until hot all the way through.

4. Meanwhile, make the sauce. Put the wine, lemon juice, shallot and 3 tablespoons of water into a small pan, bring to the boil and simmer until reduced by half. Sieve, return to the pan and simmer until reduced to 1 tablespoon. Add the cream and simmer for a bit longer, then lower the heat and gradually whisk in the butter until smooth and thick. Stir in the chopped chives and season to taste. Lift the fish cakes onto warmed plates and spoon over a little of the sauce. Serve with some steamed broccoli or spinach.

This is a deliciously simple, clean-tasting cheesecake, which we love to serve with fresh or stewed fruits, as they each come into season. Baked rhubarb and stewed gooseberries are always firm favourites.

Orange yogurt cheese cheesecake

SERVES 12

2 large, juicy navel oranges

900g Yogurt cheese
(see page 14)

250g caster sugar

3 tbsp cornflour

3 large free-range eggs,
plus 1 extra yolk

200ml crème fraîche
or soured cream

FOR THE BASE:

100g butter

200g digestive biscuits,
crushed into fine crumbs

1 tbsp demerara sugar

FOR THE TOPPING:

150g crème fraîche
or sour cream

1 tsp caster sugar

1 tsp lemon juice

1. Preheat the oven to 180°C/Gas 4. Line the base of a 24cm clip-sided tin with non-stick baking paper.

2. For the base, melt the butter in a medium-sized pan then stir in the biscuit crumbs and sugar. Spoon into the tin and press down to form a thin, even layer. Bake for 10 minutes, then remove and leave to cool. Increase the oven temperature to 240°C/Gas 9. Grease the sides of the tin with a little more butter.

3. Finely grate the zest from the oranges and squeeze the juice from 1 of them. Scoop the yogurt cheese into a bowl and beat until smooth and creamy (or use a stand mixer if you have one). Beat in the sugar, cornflour, three-quarters of the grated zest and 1 tablespoon of the orange juice, followed by the eggs, one at a time, and then the yolk. Stir in the crème fraîche or sour cream.

4. Pour the cheesecake mixture into the tin and bake for 10 minutes, then lower the oven temperature to 110°C/Gas ¼ and bake for a further 35 minutes, or until just set but still quite wobbly in the centre. Turn off the oven, leave the door ajar (wedge it open with the handle of wooden spoon if necessary) and leave inside to cool for about an hour.

5. For the topping, mix the crème fraîche or sour cream with the sugar and lemon juice. Spread over the top of the cheesecake, cover loosely with clingfilm and chill for 8 hours or overnight. Just before serving, sprinkle the remaining orange zest over the top of the cheesecake.

Caramelised oatmeal, Somerset cider brandy & honey creams with blueberries

This creamy cranachan-style pud features local brandy and blueberries in place of the typically Scottish whisky and raspberries.

SERVES 4

15g butter

50g coarse oatmeal

25g light muscovado sugar

225ml double cream

2 tbsp clear honey

50ml Somerset cider brandy

200g fresh blueberries

1. Preheat the oven to 180°C/Gas 4. Melt the butter in a small pan, stir in the oatmeal and sugar and mix together well. Spread the mixture onto a small baking tray in a thin layer and bake for 12 minutes or until golden brown. Remove and leave to cool, then crumble into small pieces with your fingers.

2. Whip the cream in a large mixing bowl until it is just beginning to thicken, then whisk in the honey and, gradually, the brandy, until the mixture holds in soft, billowy peaks. Quickly and gently, fold in three-quarters of the caramelised oatmeal and half the blueberries.

3. Drop a large spoonful of the blueberry cream into the bottom of 4 dessert glasses and scatter over half the remaining blueberries and caramelised oatmeal. Repeat once more and serve immediately.

Milk and honey jellies with honeycomb & cream

SERVES 6

1 vanilla pod

600ml whole milk

300ml double cream

18g leaf gelatine

1 jar honeycomb honey

ice-cold pouring cream, to serve

1. Slit the vanilla pod open lengthways and scrape out the seeds with the tip of a knife. Put the milk, cream, vanilla seeds and pod into a pan and bring up to the boil. Set aside for 10 minutes to infuse the milk with the flavour of vanilla, then remove the pod.

2. Meanwhile, put the gelatine leaves into a bowl of cold water and leave to soak for 5 minutes. Bring the cream almost back to the boil, then remove from the heat. Lift the gelatine out of the water, squeeze out the excess water and drop it into the hot milk. Stir until dissolved, then stir in 150g of the honey.

3. Strain the mixture into a jug and pour into 6 wetted 150ml jelly moulds, place on a tray and leave in the fridge until set — at least 4 hours.

4. To serve, dip the jelly moulds briefly into warm water and turn out onto serving plates. Place a small piece of honeycomb on top. Drizzle with a little more honey, pour a little cold cream around the plate and serve.

Don't be put off by the poppy seeds in this recipe; they add an agreeable crunch. This quick and easy cake is based on the lemon and cornflake cakes we used to make as children – see right.

Why not try... Lemon & cornflake ice-cream cake

Make the ice-cream as below but without the poppy seeds. Coarsely crush 100g cornflakes and mix together with 70g melted butter and 50g caster sugar. Spoon half the cornflake mixture into the tin and cover with the ice-cream mix. Freeze for 10–15 minutes, then add the remaining cornflakes, cover and freeze as before.

Poppy seed & lemon ice-cream cake with stewed blackcurrants

SERVES 6

4 lemons

1 x 397g can sweetened condensed milk

150ml Greek-style natural yogurt

150ml double or whipping cream

50g poppy seeds

FOR THE STEWED BLACKCURRANTS:

400g blackcurrants

150g caster sugar

1 tbsp lemon juice

1 tsp arrowroot

1. Line a 450g loaf tin with non-stick baking paper.

2. Finely grate the zest from 2 of the lemons then squeeze the juice from all 4. Pour the condensed milk into a mixing bowl and gradually beat in the lemon juice and zest. The mixture will naturally thicken. Stir in the yogurt.

3. Lightly whip the cream in a separate bowl into soft peaks and gently fold into the mixture. Stir in the poppy seeds. Pour the mixture into the prepared tin, cover with clingfilm and freeze for at least 6–8 hours (ideally overnight) until very firm.

4. Meanwhile, put the blackcurrants into a pan with the sugar and lemon juice and pop over a low heat. Cook for about 4 minutes, until the sugar has dissolved and the currants are only just starting to burst. Mix the arrowroot with 1 tablespoon cold water, stir in and simmer for 1 minute until thickened. Tip into a bowl, cool and then chill until needed.

5. To serve, remove the ice-cream from the freezer and dip the tin briefly in warm water so that you can lift it out. Leave it to soften slightly for a few minutes, then peel back the paper and cut across into 6–7mm thick slices. Serve with the stewed blackcurrants.

This recipe really is worth a go – it's so much lighter than a traditional bread pudding. Plus you'll be left with half a jar of lemon curd... a brilliant thing to have up your sleeve.

Lemon curd & raisin bread & butter pudding

SERVES 6

100g raisins

finely grated zest of 1 small lemon, plus 1 tbsp juice

1 small, fresh, tin-shaped loaf of white bread

50g soft butter

4 tbsp homemade or good lemon curd

250ml whole milk

250ml double cream

3 medium free-range eggs

25g caster sugar

icing sugar, for dusting

1. Leave the raisins to soak in the lemon juice for at least 1 hour (or overnight if you remember) so they have time to soften and soak up the juice. Preheat the oven to 190°C/Gas 5. Cut seven 5mm-thick slices of bread from the loaf, stack them up and cut off the crusts. Spread them generously with the butter and the lemon curd, then cut each one into 4 triangles.

2. Lay half of the triangles over the base of a 1.5 litre shallow ovenproof dish. Sprinkle over half the raisins, then overlap the rest of the triangles on top, butter-side up. Scatter over the remaining raisins.

3. Mix the milk, cream, eggs, sugar and lemon zest together, then pour over the top of the bread and leave to soak for 5 minutes, pushing the top layer of bread down into the liquid now and then.

4. Put the dish into a roasting tin and pour some just-boiled water from the kettle into the tin to come halfway up the sides of the dish. Bake for 30 minutes until it is puffed up and golden. Remove from the oven and the roasting tin of water. Leave to rest for a few minutes, dust with icing sugar and serve warm, with a little extra cream if you fancy.

Or you could try...

Orange & marmalade bread & butter pudding

Spread the buttered bread with fine-shred marmalade instead of lemon curd and make the custard with the zest of an orange. For a Blueberry & lemon bread & butter pudding, make the pudding as for the main recipe, replacing the lemon-soaked raisins with 150g fresh blueberries.

When we were children, each week a van would come round the village selling cakes and egg tarts. Mum wasn't too keen, so it was always a challenge to see who could run up and grab one without being spotted.

Deep-filled nutmeg & custard tart

SERVES 8-10

FOR THE PASTRY:

225g plain flour, plus extra for dusting

pinch salt

1/2 tsp fresh grated nutmeg

65g icing sugar

125g chilled butter, cut into small pieces

1 large free-range egg yolk

FOR THE FILLING:

600ml double cream

300ml whole milk

1 large vanilla pod, slit open lengthways

100g caster sugar

3 large free-range eggs, plus 3 large yolks

1¼ tsp freshly grated nutmeg

1. For the pastry, sift the flour, salt, grated nutmeg and icing sugar into a food processor. Add the butter and whiz briefly until the mixture looks like fine breadcrumbs. Beat the egg yolk briefly with 4 teaspoons cold water, add to the machine and whiz until the whole thing comes together into a ball. Turn out onto a lightly floured surface and knead briefly until smooth. Wrap in clingfilm and chill for 15 minutes, then remove from the fridge and thinly roll out. Use to line a 24cm loose-bottomed tart tin, 5cm deep. Leave to rest in the fridge for 20 minutes.

2. Preheat the oven to 200°C/Gas 6. Line the pastry case with foil and a layer of baking beans and bake on a shelf in the centre of the oven for 15 minutes. Remove the foil and beans and bake for another 5-7 minutes or until the base is crisp and golden brown. Remove and set to one side. Reduce the oven temperature to 150°C/Gas 2.

3. For the filling, put the cream, milk, vanilla pod and sugar into a pan and leave over a medium heat until just starting to bubble. Set aside and leave to infuse for 10 minutes. Meanwhile, put the eggs and egg yolks into a bowl and beat together gently.

4. Pour the hot milk over the beaten eggs, discarding the vanilla pod. Add 1 teaspoon of the grated nutmeg and mix together well. Strain the mixture through a sieve into a jug. Slide out the central oven tray, pop the tart case onto it and pour in the filling. Sprinkle over the rest of the nutmeg. Carefully slide it back into the oven and bake for 45 minutes or until the tart is just set and still quite wobbly in the centre. Remove from the oven and leave to cool. Serve warm or cold, cut into wedges.

This delicate, creamy pud just sings out summer and is great for entertaining. Most of the bits can be prepared in advance and assembled just before serving. Very handy indeed.

Floating islands with red summer berries

SERVES 6

450g mixed red summer berries (redcurrants, raspberries and sliced small strawberries)

FOR THE CARAMEL:

75g caster sugar

1 tbsp kirsch

FOR THE CUSTARD:

400ml whole milk

100ml double cream

1 vanilla pod, slit open lengthways and seeds scraped out

6 large free-range egg yolks

50g caster sugar

2 tbsp kirsch

FOR THE SOFT MERINGUES:

2 large free-range egg whites

50g caster sugar

1. For the caramel, warm the sugar and 2 tablespoons water in a small pan over a low heat until the sugar has dissolved and the syrup is clear. Turn up the heat and boil until it goes a deep amber-colour, then whip off the heat and plunge the pan's base into cold water. Carefully add the kirsch and 2 further tablespoons water. Return to a low heat and stir until all the caramel bits have dissolved, then leave to cool. Pour into a jug, cover and set aside until needed.

2. For the custard, put the milk, cream, vanilla seeds and pod into a pan, bring the boil then set aside for 10 minutes. Fish out the pod. Whisk the egg yolks and sugar together in a bowl until pale and creamy, return the milk mixture to the boil and gradually whisk it into the egg yolks. Pour the lot back into the pan and cook over a low heat, stirring constantly, until the mixture thickens and coats the back of a wooden spoon. Sieve into a clean bowl and stir in the kirsch. Leave to cool, then cover and chill for at least 4 hours or until needed.

3. Shortly before serving, make the meringues. Bring 500ml water to a very gentle simmer in a large frying pan. Whisk the egg whites in a clean bowl until white and foamy, add half the sugar and whisk into soft peaks. Gradually whisk in the remaining sugar to form a stiff and glossy meringue. Scoop out a large spoonful of the meringue and gently ease it onto the surface of the water. Form 2 more 'islands' and leave them to poach for 3 minutes. Lift out with a slotted spoon onto a baking tray lined with a clean tea towel and repeat to make another 3 'islands'.

4. To serve, pour the custard into the base of 6 glass dishes or bowls. Float one of the meringue islands on top. Scatter some of the berries around each island and drizzle over a little of the caramel to finish.

This is one of the most popular treats at our tea rooms. We make it with summer fruits as they appear. All you need on the side is a good strong cup of tea.

Raspberry, lemon & yogurt tea loaf

MAKES ONE 1KG LOAF

250g plain flour

2 tsp baking powder

pinch salt

115g soft butter

225g caster sugar

finely grated zest
and juice of 1 large lemon

2 large free-range eggs

100g wholemilk natural yogurt

25g ground almonds

200g fresh raspberries

100g granulated sugar,
plus extra for sprinkling

1. Preheat the oven to 180°C/Gas 4. Grease and line a 900g loaf tin with non-stick baking paper.

2. Sift together the flour, baking powder and salt. Cream together the butter and caster sugar in a large mixing bowl for 5 minutes until pale and fluffy, then beat in the lemon zest. Beat in the eggs, one at a time, adding a tablespoon of the sifted flour with the second egg. Alternately fold in large spoonfuls of the remaining flour and the yogurt until the mixture is smooth, then fold in the ground almonds.

3. Spoon a third of the cake mixture into the bottom of the loaf tin and scatter over a third of the raspberries. Repeat twice more, ending with a layer of raspberries. Bake for 45—50 minutes until the cake is nicely browned, then cover loosely with foil and bake for a further 20—25 minutes, until a skewer inserted into the middle of the cake comes away clean.

4. Remove the cake from the oven and leave it to cool for 5 minutes. Mix the granulated sugar with the lemon juice, spoon it over the top of the cake and leave it to soak for 5 minutes. Carefully remove the cake from the tin and pop it on a wire rack to cool.

5. Peel the paper away from the cake and sprinkle the top lightly with a little more sugar. Serve cut into thick slices.

Why not try...?

Making this cake with fresh blackberries or blueberries instead of raspberries.

the farmhouse kitchen

Ah, baking... surely the most generous of kitchen activities. Most people don't really bake for themselves but for others, and we're the same. Yes, we love the smells and anticipation of a homemade cake. And the licking of the bowl. But more than that, for us, baking is about sharing the love, both with family and friends. Might sound a bit soppy but it's true.

We're not scientists, but we reckon there's a pretty clear link between baking talent and popularity. Just something we've noticed.

Out of all the different types of cooking, baking has to be the best one to get the children involved in.

What could be better on a Sunday afternoon than raiding the cupboard for flour and eggs and making a good old mess?

And then there's the suspense as it's baking in the oven. Will it rise? Will it be moist and delicious? Hopefully with the following recipes the answer is 'yes!'

Choc chip cookies

1. Sift together 225g plain flour, ½ tsp baking powder and ½ tsp salt. Mix 60g cocoa powder together with 100g melted butter in a large bowl until very smooth. Stir in 450g caster sugar, 1 tsp vanilla extract and 160ml butter milk, then gradually stir in the flour mixture and 150g chocolate chips.

2. Drop heaped teaspoons of the biscuit dough onto 2 lined baking sheets, leaving about 5cm between each one. Bake in a pre heated oven at 180C/Gas 4 for 7-9 minutes, until set and lightly coloured. Leave to cool for 2-3 minutes, then transfer to a wire rack and leave to cool completely.

Crunchy apple & raspberry granola

MAKES APPROX. 10 SERVINGS

125g organic jumbo oats

125g organic porridge oats

35g each blanched whole almonds, skinned hazelnuts and walnut pieces

2 tbsp sesame seeds

25g sunflower seeds

25g pumpkin seeds

50ml rapeseed, grapeseed or sunflower oil

50g clear honey

50g light soft brown sugar

2 tbsp light tahini paste

25g flaked dried coconut

50g dried apples or pears, chopped into raisin-sized pieces

25g each dried cranberries, blueberries and sour cherries

15g freeze-dried raspberries

1. Preheat the oven to 170°C/Gas 3. Pop the oats, nuts and seeds in a mixing bowl and mix together well. Warm the oil, honey, sugar and tahini paste together in a small pan until smooth and runny, add to the dry ingredients and mix well, then scrunch the whole lot together a little with your hands to encourage the mixture to stick together in small clumps.

2. Spread the mixture evenly over a large baking tray lined with greaseproof paper and bake for 20 minutes, lifting and turning the mixture over after 10 minutes, then every 5 minutes or so after that, taking care not to break up the lumps. Scatter over the flaked coconut and bake for a further 5 minutes, by which time everything should be lightly golden. Remove from the oven and leave to cool. Mix together the dried fruits.

3. Store both mixes separately in airtight containers until needed (they will keep for about a month). Stir them together before serving and serve with lashings of natural yogurt and/or seasonal fruit compotes.

Apple & honey bircher muesli with fruit & nuts

SERVES 6

225g organic porridge oats

200ml pressed apple juice

225g wholemilk natural yogurt

50g clear honey

finely grated zest of 1 small lemon

2 dessert apples, quartered, cored and coarsely grated

A CHOICE OF TOPPINGS:

225g chopped apples & 50g lightly toasted walnut pieces

225g blueberries & 50g lightly toasted hazelnuts, coarsely chopped

225g raspberries & 50g lightly toasted pecan nut pieces

225g chopped pears & 50g toasted unblanched almonds, coarsely chopped

1. Mix the porridge oats, 200ml cold water and the apple juice together in a bowl. Cover with clingfilm and chill overnight.

2. The next morning, stir in the yogurt, honey, lemon zest and grated apples. Spoon into individual bowls and sprinkle with the topping of your choice.

Our children love making these pancakes; well, they're so simple to cook. Feel free to sprinkle some fresh fruit over them while they're frying. Raspberries and strawberries work well, as do slices of banana.

Buttermilk pancakes with honey & vanilla butter

SERVES 4

100g self-raising flour

1 tsp baking powder

25g caster sugar

pinch salt

2 large free-range eggs, separated

175ml buttermilk

40ml whole milk

45g butter, melted and cooled

FOR THE HONEY & VANILLA BUTTER:

100g soft butter

3 tbsp clear honey

1 tsp vanilla bean paste

1. For the butter, simply beat the ingredients together with an electric whisk until pale and creamy. Spoon into a small bowl and leave to firm up slightly in the fridge for 1 hour.

2. For the pancakes, sift the flour, baking powder, sugar and salt into a bowl. Make a well in the middle and add the egg yolks, buttermilk, milk and 15g of the melted butter. Whisk together to make a smooth batter. Pop the egg whites into a large clean bowl and whisk into soft peaks, then gently fold into the batter.

3. Heat a large non-stick frying pan over a medium heat. Brush the base with a little of the melted butter. Add 3-4 large spoonfuls of the batter, spaced well apart, to the pan and cook for 2 minutes until bubbles start to appear in the top of the mixture, and they are golden brown underneath. Turn over and cook for 1 minute more. Serve in batches as you cook them or put them onto a plate, cover with a clean tea towel and keep warm in a low oven while you cook the remainder. Serve hot with the honey and vanilla butter.

Or you could try...

Ricotta pancakes. Replace half the buttermilk with 175g ricotta cheese. Serve with sliced raw or pan-fried bananas and the vanilla and honey butter.

Bacon & maple syrup pancakes. This might sound weird but in Holland they love to serve pancakes with maple syrup and crispy bacon. Give it a go — it's a great combination of salty and sweet.

Farls are very similar to soda bread, but the mixture is cut into wedges before cooking. This recipe will make eight farls, so serve one or two per person. Hungry farmers tend to polish off two each with no problem.

Cheddar farls with fried eggs & crispy bacon

SERVES 4

FOR THE FARLS:

450g self-raising flour, plus extra for kneading

1 tsp bicarbonate of soda

1 tsp English mustard powder

2 tsp yellow mustard seeds, lightly crushed

150g cheddar, finely grated

280ml buttermilk, mixed with 90ml whole milk

salt and freshly ground black pepper

TO SERVE:

4 strings of cherry tomatoes on the vine

a little olive oil

12 rashers dry-cured streaky bacon, smoked or unsmoked

4 large free-range eggs

sunflower oil, for shallow frying

butter, for spreading

1. Preheat the oven to 220°C/Gas 7. Sift the flour, bicarb, 1 teaspoon salt and mustard powder together into a bowl and stir in the mustard seeds and cheddar. Make a well in the centre, add the buttermilk mixture and mix together into a soft, slightly sticky dough.

2. Turn the dough out onto a lightly floured surface and very quickly and gently shape it into a 22cm round. Lift it onto a lightly floured non-stick baking sheet and cut into 8 wedges. Separate the wedges to give them room to rise and spread, sprinkle with a bit more flour and bake for 20 minutes until golden brown.

3. While the farls are cooking, put the strings of cherry tomatoes into a small roasting tin, drizzle with a little olive oil and season lightly. After the farls have been cooking for 10 minutes, slide the tin of tomatoes alongside and roast for 10 minutes.

4. Meanwhile, pop a griddle over a high heat until smoking, reduce the heat to medium and cook the bacon until crisp and golden. At the same time, shallow fry the eggs until done to your liking. (We like ours with the edges crispy but the yolks still runny.)

5. Remove the farls from the oven, slice them in half and spread with butter. Fill with the bacon rashers, top with the eggs and serve with the tomatoes.

Or how about...?

Spring onion & yogurt farls. Add 8–10 sliced spring onions to the dry mixture and use 140g wholemilk natural yogurt mixed with 140ml milk in place of the buttermilk.

OK, major top tip coming up. If you want to make the lightest scones ever, we have a secret ingredient for you: yogurt. Something to do with the way it reacts with the baking powder. These beauties always go down a storm at our tea room.

White chocolate, yogurt & sour cherry scones

MAKES 12 SCONES

450g self-raising flour

large pinch salt

4 tsp baking powder

100g chilled butter, diced

50g caster sugar

150g dried sour cherries, halved

150g white chocolate chunks or chips for cooking

2 medium free-range eggs

100g wholemilk natural yogurt

approx. 200ml whole milk

granulated sugar, for sprinkling

1. Preheat the oven to 220°C/Gas 7. Sift the flour, salt and baking powder into the bowl of a food processor, add the butter and whiz until the mixture looks like fine breadcrumbs. Tip into a mixing bowl and stir in the caster sugar, cherries and chocolate.

2. Put the eggs and yogurt into a measuring jug and make up to 400ml with the milk. Make a well in the centre of the dried ingredients, add all but 2 tablespoons of the milky mixture and very lightly mix to make a soft, slightly sticky dough. Don't over mix!

3. Turn the dough out onto a lightly floured surface and knead very lightly and briefly, until just smooth. Then lightly pat out the dough until it is about 3cm thick. Cut out as many scones as you can using a floured 7cm cutter. Gently re-knead and pat out the trimmings twice more to make a total of 12 scones.

4. Place the scones, slightly apart, on a large greased baking sheet and brush with the remaining milky mixture. Sprinkle with a little granulated sugar and bake for 12-15 minutes until puffed up, golden brown and cooked through.

5. Lift onto a wire rack and leave to cool, then eat as soon as possible with lashings of butter and jam.

Or you could try...

Cranberry & orange scones. Use 150g dried cranberries mixed with 100g chopped candied orange or mixed peel instead of the chocolate/cherries and add the finely grated zest of an orange to the egg mix.

This is a lovely, moist cake, partly thanks to yesterday's newspaper. Tying a thick band around the tin before it goes in the oven helps stop the outside cooking too quickly and drying out.

Somerset scrumpy & apple cake

MAKES ONE 23CM CAKE

215g plain flour

15g cornflour

1½ tsp baking powder

½ tsp salt

¼ tsp ground cinnamon

¼ tsp ground cloves

¼ tsp ground ginger

¼ tsp freshly grated nutmeg

300g caster sugar,
plus extra for sprinkling

175g soft unsalted butter

2 medium free-range eggs

3 tbsp cider or scrumpy

450g peeled and cored dessert apples, cut into 1cm pieces

75g raisins

100g lightly toasted walnuts, broken into small pieces

1. Preheat the oven to 180°C/Gas 4. Grease and line a 23cm round, loose-bottomed cake tin with non-stick baking paper. Tie a thick band of folded newspaper around the outside of the tin and secure with string.

2. Sift the flour, cornflour, baking powder, salt and spices into the bowl of a stand mixer. Add the sugar and butter and beat together on a medium-speed for 1 minute until well mixed.

3. Add the eggs and mix on a low speed for a few seconds, then increase the speed and beat for 1 minute until light and fluffy. Beat in the cider.

4. Fold in the prepared apples, raisins and walnuts. The mixture will look very thick, but don't worry. Spoon it into the prepared tin and level the surface.

5. Bake for about 1¼ hours, covering the cake loosely with foil once it is richly browned on top, until firm to the touch and a skewer inserted into the centre of it comes away clean. Leave to cool in the tin on a wire rack, then remove from the tin to a plate, sprinkle with caster sugar and serve.

Or how about...?

Pear, pecan and date cake. Use firm, ripe pears instead of the apples, pecan nuts instead of the walnuts and chopped soft dried dates instead of the raisins. This cake is also lovely made with soft light brown sugar instead of caster sugar.

When we were little, we'd run out to the fields with thick slices of this cake for all the people making hay. We still remember the joy on their faces as they munched away, sitting on top of the bales.

Farmhouse fruit cake

MAKES ONE 23CM CAKE

550g mixed dried fruit
(we like raisins, cranberries, blueberries, sour cherries and chopped candied peel)

450g self-raising flour

1½ tsp mixed spice

large pinch salt

300g soft butter

300g caster sugar

4 medium free-range eggs

200ml whole milk

2 tbsp demerara sugar

1. Put the mixed dried fruit into a bowl with 120ml hot water. Stir together well and leave to soak for 1 hour, stirring now and then. Meanwhile, grease and line a 23cm deep, round, loose-bottomed cake tin with non-stick baking paper. Make a deep band from a few folded sheets of newspaper and tie it around the outside of the tin.

2. Preheat the oven to 150°C/Gas 2. Spread the soaked dried fruits out onto a clean tea towel and dry well. Tip into a bowl, toss with 2 tablespoons of the flour and set aside. Sift the remaining flour into a separate bowl with the mixed spice and salt.

3. Cream the butter and caster sugar together for 5 minutes until pale and fluffy. Beat in the eggs, one at a time, adding 1 tablespoon of the sifted flour with the last 2 eggs. Fold in the rest of the flour in 2 batches, alternating with the milk, until smooth, then fold in the dried fruits.

4. Spoon the mixture into the tin and lightly level the top, then sprinkle over the demerara sugar. Bake the cake in the centre of the oven for about 1¾ hours, until a skewer inserted into the cake comes away clean, and it has just started to show signs of shrinking away from the sides of the tin. Leave the cake to cool in the tin for 5 minutes, then remove and leave to cool on a wire rack.

If you've never tried a blondie, all we can say is you really must. They're like brownies but, well, blonde. That'll be the white chocolate! These ones are also wonderful served warm with ice-cream.

Or how about...?
Dark chocolate and raspberry brownies
Melt 250g butter with 250g of 70% dark chocolate. Whisk the eggs, sugar and vanilla as before and fold in the melted chocolate, 50g ground almonds and 100g raspberries. Pour the mixture into the prepared tin, scatter another 100g raspberries on top and bake for 30–35 minutes.

Redcurrant & white chocolate blondies

MAKES 16

250g good white chocolate

125g butter

4 large free-range eggs

350g caster sugar

2 tsp vanilla extract

150g plain flour

½ tsp salt

150g ground almonds

200g fresh redcurrants, stripped from their stalks

icing sugar, for dusting (optional)

1. Grease and line a rectangular 20 x 30cm cake tin or brownie pan with non-stick baking paper. Preheat the oven to 170°C/Gas 3.

2. Put the white chocolate and butter into a heatproof bowl, sit it over a pan of barely simmering water and melt very gently, stirring regularly until smooth. (Take care not to let it get too hot or it will 'seize' and go grainy.) Set aside to cool slightly.

3. Beat the eggs, sugar and vanilla extract together, in a stand mixer or by hand, for 10 minutes until really thick and moussy. Gently fold in the melted chocolate, then sift over and fold in the flour and salt. Fold in the ground almonds and redcurrants.

4. Pour the mixture into the prepared tin and bake for 35–40 minutes, until firm and shiny on top and a skewer pushed into the centre of the cake comes away with some very sticky crumbs clinging to it.

5. Leave to cool in the tin for 10 minutes or so, then carefully lift it onto a cooling rack and leave to go cold. Cut into squares and dust with icing sugar if you wish.

Honeycomb might seem rather an odd thing to make yourself but it's actually really easy, and good fun. The way it fizzes up when you add the bicarb – wonderful!

Honeycomb & chocolate biscuit cake

MAKES APPROX. 24 PIECES

115ml double cream

600g good plain chocolate (70% cocoa solids), broken into pieces

165g butter

100g dried sour cherries, blueberries or raisins

75g (approx. 9) Savoiardi biscuits, cut into 2.5cm pieces

cocoa powder, for dusting

FOR THE HONEYCOMB:

500g caster sugar

125g liquid glucose

100g clear honey

1 tbsp bicarbonate of soda, loaded into a tea strainer ready for sifting

1. For the honeycomb, lightly oil and line a 20 x 30cm loaf tin with non-stick baking paper, making sure the paper comes at least 5cm above the edges. Put the sugar, glucose, honey and 90ml water in a large pan over a low heat and stir gently until the sugar has dissolved and the syrup is clear. Bring to the boil, put a sugar thermometer into the pan and leave to boil rapidly without stirring until it reaches 150°C.

2. When the sugar syrup reaches the right temperature, turn off the heat, quickly sift over the bicarbonate of soda and whisk in vigorously. The mixture will froth up, become lighter and start rising up the sides of the pan. As it reaches the top, pour it into the tin. Leave it for 30 minutes to go cold and become brittle.

3. Lightly oil and line a 20cm square shallow tin with non-stick baking paper. Put 85ml of the cream, 450g of the chocolate and 125g of the butter into a medium-sized pan and the remaining cream, chocolate and butter into another smaller pan. Stir the larger pan of mixture over a low heat until it has melted.

4. Put 150g of the honeycomb in a plastic bag and break into raisin-sized pieces with a rolling pin. Put into a bowl with the fruit and biscuits, then pour over the melted chocolate mixture and stir together. Scoop it into the tin, spread it out to the edges and level the top.

5. Gently melt the remaining chocolate mixture, pour it into the tin and spread out evenly to fill out any gaps. Chill in the fridge for 3 hours or until set. Remove from the tin, cut lengthways in half and across into fingers, dust with cocoa powder and leave to soften slightly before serving.

These delicious fingers are kind of like posh bakewell tarts. They're a great way to use up any leftover jam you might have lurking in the back of your cupboards.

Blackberry & brown sugar fingers

MAKES 16 FINGERS

FOR THE BASE:

225g soft butter

75g sifted icing sugar

225g plain flour

50g cornflour

pinch salt

200g blackberry jam

FOR THE TOPPING:

125g soft butter

125g light muscovado sugar

finely grated zest of 1 lemon

2 large free-range eggs, beaten

25g self-raising flour

175g ground almonds

200g blackberries

25g flaked almonds

1 tbsp demerara sugar, plus extra for sprinkling

1. Preheat the oven to 180°C/Gas 4. Grease and line a 20 x 30cm loose-bottomed brownie tin with non-stick baking paper.

2. For the base, cream the butter and icing sugar together in a bowl until pale and fluffy. Sift over the flour, cornflour and salt and stir into the butter mixture to make a soft, shortbread-like dough. Roll the dough out on a lightly floured surface almost to the size of the tin, lower into the tin and press out a little to the edges. Prick here and there with a fork and bake for 16 minutes until a pale biscuit colour. Remove and leave to go cold, then carefully spread with the jam to within 1cm of the edges.

3. For the topping, cream the butter and muscovado sugar together until light and fluffy. Beat in the lemon zest. Gradually beat in the beaten eggs, then fold in the flour and ground almonds. Dollop small spoonfuls of mixture over the jam and carefully spread it out in an even layer. Scatter over the blackberries, pushing half of them down into the mix.

4. Sprinkle over the tablespoon of demerara sugar and bake for 10 minutes. Carefully slide out the oven shelf, sprinkle over the flaked almonds and bake for another 30 minutes, or until golden brown and a skewer pushed into the topping comes out clean. Remove, sprinkle with a little more demerara sugar and leave to cool in the tin. Then cut lengthways in half, and across into 16 fingers.

Ginger cake and parkin are two of our favourite wintertime treats. This easy-to-make recipe is made extra moreish by virtue of some rather special fudge-like frosting.

Ginger cake with fudgy frosting

MAKES 1 X 23CM SQUARE CAKE

225g butter

225g dark muscovado sugar

200g golden syrup

1 tbsp black treacle

2 large free-range eggs, beaten

300ml whole milk

375g plain flour

large pinch salt

2 tsp bicarbonate of soda

2 tsp ground ginger

FOR THE FUDGY FROSTING:

75g butter

180ml double cream

75g caster sugar

75g light muscovado sugar

pinch salt

1. Preheat the oven to 150°C/Gas 2. Grease and line a 23cm square cake tin with non-stick baking paper.

2. Put the butter, sugar, syrup and treacle into a pan and stir over a low heat until melted. Leave to cool slightly, then stir in the eggs and milk.

3. Sift the flour, salt, bicarb and ground ginger into a mixing bowl and make a well in the centre. Add the liquid mixture and beat together until smooth.

4. Pour the batter into the tin and bake for about 1 hour or until well risen and firm to the touch. Leave to cool in the tin for 10 minutes, then turn out and leave to go cold on a cooling rack.

5. For the frosting, put the ingredients into a medium-sized pan and stir over a medium heat until melted. Bring to the boil and simmer for 5 minutes, stirring now and then. Remove from the heat and beat with a wooden spoon until the mixture has thickened to a toffee sauce-like consistency. Leave to cool completely, beating occasionally to prevent it forming a sugary skin. When cold beat vigorously, until thick and spreadable.

6. Spoon the frosting onto the top of the cake and spread out in an even layer, then swirl with the blade of the knife. Leave to set completely before cutting into slices to serve.

MAKES 2 SMALL LOAVES

400g stoneground wholemeal flour

200g plain white flour,
plus a little extra for flouring

1 rounded tsp bicarbonate of soda

1 tsp salt

approx. 600ml buttermilk

Living on a farm and making bread seem to go hand in hand. Don't panic if the dough seems sticky, this is how it should be. Avoid adding extra flour: hold your nerve, knead gently and you'll be rewarded with a delightfully moist loaf.

Stoneground soda bread

1. Preheat the oven to 230°C/Gas 8.

2. Mix the flours, bicarb and salt together in a large mixing bowl.
   Make a well in the centre, pour in most of the buttermilk and
   mix together, adding a little more buttermilk if necessary,
   until it comes together into a soft, sticky dough.

3. Turn the dough out onto a lightly floured surface and knead
   very lightly and briefly until it comes together into a ball.
   Cut the dough in half and knead each piece briefly once more
   into a smooth round. Do not over-knead the mixture, as this
   will make the bread very heavy. Slightly flatten each round
   into 4cm-thick discs. Place them well apart on a baking sheet
   lightly dusted with flour, then, using a large, sharp knife,
   cut a large, deep cross into the top of each loaf, to within
   about 1cm of the base.

4. Bake the loaves on the middle shelf of the oven for 15 minutes,
   then lower the oven temperature to 200°C/Gas 6 and bake for
   another 10 minutes, until they are well risen and have developed
   a rich, golden brown crust. They should also sound hollow when
   you tap their bases. Leave to cool on a wire rack. Eat on the
   same day as baking.

Or you could try...

Cheesy oat bread. Replace 25g of the wholemeal flour with
porridge oats and stir 75g coarsely grated cheddar into the
dry flour mixture. Before you cut the cross into the top of
the loaf, sprinkle it with another 50g grated cheese and
a few more oats. **Rosemary & olive bread.** Add 2 tbsp chopped
rosemary and 100g roughly chopped pitted green olives
to the dry flour mixture. **Sun-dried tomato & thyme bread.**
Add 100g coarsely chopped sun-dried tomatoes 2 tbsp picked
thyme leaves to the dry flour mixture.

This is an unusual but wonderful bread,
which we make with our homemade cider.
Studded with lovely dried fruits and nuts,
it goes really well with soup or some good cheese.

Somerset cider, honey, walnut & raisin bread

MAKES 2 LARGE LOAVES

175g raisins

500g strong white bread flour, plus extra for flouring

500g stoneground wholemeal flour

10g easy-blend yeast

20g salt

2 tbsp clear honey

500ml dry cider

200g lightly toasted walnut pieces

1. Cover the raisins with 50ml boiling water and soak overnight. Drain and pat dry with kitchen paper.

2. Put the flours, yeast and salt into a large mixing bowl or the bowl of a stand mixer. Warm the honey, cider and 200ml water in a small pan, add to the bowl and mix everything together into a dough. Knead the dough for 10 minutes until smooth and elastic, then pop it in a lightly oiled bowl, cover tightly with oiled clingfilm and a tea towel and leave somewhere warm to rise for 1–2 hours until doubled in size.

3. Turn the dough out onto a lightly floured surface or into the bowl of the stand mixer and knead for 2–3 minutes, then knead in the raisins and walnuts. Divide the dough in half and knead each piece into a neat round, then put each loaf onto a well-floured baking tray. Cover again with oiled clingfilm and a tea towel and leave to rise once more until doubled in size.

4. Preheat the oven to its highest temperature. 5 minutes before baking, put a small roasting tray of boiling hot water into the base of the oven.

5. Put the loaves onto the middle shelf of the oven and bake for 10 minutes. Lower the oven temperature to 180°C/Gas 4 and bake for a further 20 minutes until they are nicely browned and sound hollow when tapped on the base. Leave to cool on a wire rack.

Or you could try…

Quick rye bread. Replace the wholemeal flour with rye flour. Use 25g caraway seeds instead of the honey, raisins and walnuts, and use just water for the dough.

Oh, how we love the quince. Unspeakably hard and tart when raw, but when cooked: sweet, sumptuous and fragrant. It's also the fruit that gave marmalade its name – 'marmelo' being Portuguese for 'quince'.

Quince & orange marmalade

MAKES APPROX. 6 X 400G JARS

450g ordinary oranges
(not Seville)

1.35kg ripe quinces,
peeled and cored

1.35kg granulated sugar

1. Pare the zest from the oranges with a sharp potato peeler, leaving behind as much of the white pith as you can. Cut each strip lengthways into fine shreds. Halve the fruit, squeeze out the juice and set aside.

2. Put the prepared quince into a food processor fitted with the coarse shredding blade and whiz into strips. Put them into a bowl and stir in the orange juice.

3. Sterilise your jars as on page 72 and pop a few saucers in the freezer to chill. Put the zest and 1.5 litres water in a preserving pan or large saucepan and simmer for 20 minutes. Add the quince mixture, return to the boil and simmer for 5 minutes, until tender.

4. Add the sugar to the pan and stir over a low heat until completely dissolved. Bring the mixture to a rapid boil and boil until setting point is reached. (This will take between 20 and 30 minutes, depending on the ripeness of your fruit.) After 15 minutes, draw the pan off the heat, spoon a little of the marmalade onto one of the chilled saucers and return to the freezer for a few minutes until cold. Push your finger across the surface — if it wrinkles into a peak with no liquid running back it's done. If not, continue to boil, testing at 3 minute intervals.

5. As soon as setting point has been reached, remove the pan from the heat, stir to disperse any scum, and leave to settle and cool slightly for 20 minutes.

6. Skim any scum from the surface, then ladle into the hot sterilised jars, filling them to within 6mm of the top. Press a waxed disc onto the marmalade's surface and seal with lids while still hot. Label and store in a cool dark place. It will keep for at least 2 years.

This is one of our favourite flavour combinations:
the tang of the rhubarb, the sweetness of the
strawberries... wonderful! The rhubarb also has a
practical role – the pectin inside helps the jam to set.

Strawberry & rhubarb jam

MAKES 7-8 X 350G JARS

1kg young, trimmed
rhubarb stalks, wiped clean

1kg small strawberries,
washed and hulled

6 tbsp lemon juice

1.8kg jam sugar

15g unsalted butter

1. Cut the rhubarb into 2cm pieces. Put into a large bowl with the strawberries, lemon juice and sugar and stir together well. Cover with a tea towel and leave somewhere cool but not in the fridge, overnight. This will draw out some of the juices from the fruit and help to keep the strawberries whole during cooking.

2. The next day, put 3 or 4 saucers into the freezer and prepare your jam jars. Preheat the oven to 150°C/Gas 2. Wash your jars and lids in hot soapy water, rinse well and drain briefly. Transfer to the oven and leave for at least 15 minutes before using.

3. Transfer the fruit mixture to a preserving pan or large, deep saucepan (of at least 4.5 litre capacity) and heat gently, stirring frequently, until the sugar has completely dissolved. Add the butter and bring to a rolling boil.

4. Boil the jam rapidly for 8-10 minutes, until it reaches between 104-105°C, then draw the pan off the heat and check for setting point. Spoon a little jam onto one of the chilled saucers, return it to the freezer and leave for 2 minutes. Then push your finger through it. If it wrinkles up into a peak with no liquid running back onto the saucer, it's ready. If it doesn't, boil for another 2-3 minutes and re-test. Remove from the heat, skim off any scum and leave to cool for 15-20 minutes or until the fruit stays suspended in the jam after you've stirred it. If you pot your jam too early the fruit will just float back to the surface.

5. Ladle the jam into the warm, sterilised jars using a jam funnel, cover immediately with waxed discs and lids, then label and date. It will keep in a cool dry place for up to 6 months.

the veg garden

A few years ago, Sarah Mead, Tim's wife, breathed new life into our organic gardens, transforming them into one of the most beautiful and fascinating parts of the farm. This is where we grow lots of lovely vegetables, everything from broad beans to beetroot – most of them destined for dishes served at our HQ and tea room.

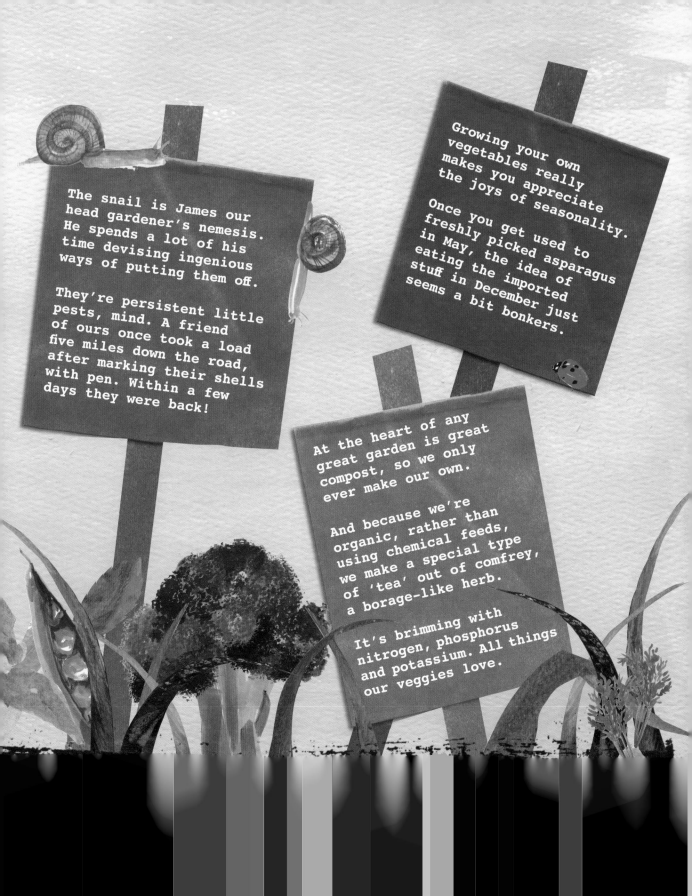

The snail is James our head gardener's nemesis. He spends a lot of his time devising ingenious ways of putting them off.

They're persistent little pests, mind. A friend of ours once took a load five miles down the road, after marking their shells with pen. Within a few days they were back!

Growing your own vegetables really makes you appreciate the joys of seasonality.

Once you get used to freshly picked asparagus in May, the idea of eating the imported stuff in December just seems a bit bonkers.

At the heart of any great garden is great compost, so we only ever make our own.

And because we're organic, rather than using chemical feeds, we make a special type of 'tea' out of comfrey, a borage-like herb.

It's brimming with nitrogen, phosphorus and potassium. All things our veggies love.

The key to this recipe is to use super-fresh eggs.
That way the whites will stay together beautifully
as you poach them. The farmers' market is always
a good bet for eggs, as they're normally days rather
than weeks old.

Cream of asparagus soup with soft-poached eggs

SERVES 4

600g fine asparagus

1 litre good vegetable
or chicken stock

½ tsp white wine vinegar

4 large, really fresh
free-range eggs

65g unsalted butter

150g leeks, white part only,
trimmed and thinly sliced

2 small celery stalks,
thinly sliced

30g plain flour

1½ tbsp double cream

salt and freshly ground
black pepper

1. Rinse the asparagus, snap off the woody ends and roughly chop them. Put the chopped ends in a pan with the stock, bring to the boil, cover and simmer for 15 minutes. Strain, discarding the ends, and set the stock aside.

2. Meanwhile, cut the tips off the asparagus spears and halve lengthwise. Roughly chop the remaining stalks. Bring 2 small pans of lightly salted water to the boil. Drop the asparagus tips into one pan and cook for 2 minutes until just tender. Drain, refresh under cold water and set aside. Add the vinegar to the second pan and lower the heat. Swirl the water with a spoon to make a whirlpool, crack in an egg and poach for 3 minutes, then carefully remove with a slotted spoon and set aside on kitchen paper. Repeat with the remaining eggs, leaving the water to simmer.

3. Melt 50g of the butter in a large pan, add the asparagus stalks, sliced leeks and celery, cover and cook over a low heat for 10 minutes until soft but not browned.

4. Uncover, stir in the flour and cook for a further minute. Stir in the asparagus-flavoured stock, cover again and simmer for 10 minutes until the veg are tender. Remove from the heat, cool slightly, then liquidise the soup in batches until smooth. Pass through a sieve back into a clean pan, bring back to a simmer and stir in the cream. Season to taste.

5. Melt the remaining butter. Lower the eggs back into the simmering water and leave for 30 seconds. Remove and drain on kitchen paper. Ladle the soup into warmed bowls and scatter over the asparagus tips. Place a poached egg into each bowl, season to taste, drizzle over the melted butter and serve.

This is an excellent soup for dealing with a glut of tomatoes, should you be lucky enough to have that problem. It's delicious with some basil pesto or black olive tapenade swirled through just before serving.

Slow-roasted tomato soup with chilli & cheese cornmeal muffins

SERVES 6–8

1.75kg tomatoes

150ml olive oil,
plus extra for garnish

4 large garlic cloves, chopped

the leaves from 3 large thyme
sprigs, plus extra to garnish

the leaves from 3 x 18cm
rosemary sprigs

3 medium onions,
halved and thinly sliced

3 fat celery stalks, sliced

1/2 tsp fennel seeds,
lightly crushed

1/2 tsp crushed dried chillies

1.2 litres good vegetable
or light chicken stock

1 tbsp tomato purée

2 tsp caster sugar

juice of 1 lime

salt and freshly
ground black pepper

FOR THE MUFFINS:

115g plain flour

1 tbsp baking powder

1/4 tsp salt

100g dried polenta

85g cheddar, finely grated

1/4 tsp crushed dried chillies

1 medium free-range
egg, beaten

175ml whole milk

50g butter, melted

1. Preheat the oven to 190°C/Gas 5. Halve the tomatoes and lay them cut-side up in a single layer in a large, lightly oiled roasting tin. Sprinkle with salt, pepper and a few tablespoons of oil and roast for 45 minutes–1 hour, depending on their size, until they have shrivelled and concentrated in flavour.

2. Meanwhile, pour the remaining oil into a large pan and add the garlic, thyme and rosemary. Place over a medium heat and as soon as everything is sizzling nicely, add the onions, celery, fennel seeds and dried chilli. Stir well, cover and cook over a low heat for 20 minutes, uncovering and stirring once or twice, until the onion is very soft but not browned.

3. Add 600ml of the stock, bring to a simmer and cook, covered, for 10 more minutes. Uncover, add the tomatoes and juices from the tin, the tomato purée and sugar and simmer for 2–3 minutes. Remove from the heat, leave to cool slightly, then liquidise in batches until smooth. Sieve into a clean pan and stir in enough stock to give the soup a good consistency.

4. For the muffins, increase the oven to 200°C/Gas 6. Line a muffin tray with 8 deep non-stick paper cases. Sift the flour, baking powder and salt into a mixing bowl and stir in the polenta, 75g of the grated cheese and the dried chillies. Make a well in the centre, add the egg, milk and melted butter and mix everything together, then spoon into the paper cases. Sprinkle with the remaining grated cheese and bake in the oven for 20 minutes until well-risen and golden.

5. Shortly before the muffins are ready, gently reheat the soup. Add the lime juice and season to taste with salt and pepper. Serve with the muffins.

SERVES 8

450g freshly shelled broad beans

10g basil leaves, torn into pieces

50g finely grated pecorino

2 tbsp extra-virgin olive oil

1 tsp lemon juice

salt and freshly
ground black pepper

TO SERVE:

1 x 250g buffalo mozzarella
(drained weight)

16 small slices of bread

1 large garlic clove, peeled and halved

25g wild rocket leaves

lemon-infused extra-virgin olive oil

sea salt flakes

We serve these lovely little toasts at our garden parties and picnics. They also make a fab starter for barbecues.

Broad bean pâté on toast with torn mozzarella, basil, & lemon oil

1. Drop the broad beans into a pan of well-salted boiling water and cook for 2–3 minutes until just tender. Drain, run under cold water to cool, then nick the skin of each bean with your fingernail and pop the bright green beans out of their skins.

2. Put the skinned beans and torn basil leaves into the bowl of a food processor and briefly blitz into a coarse paste. Stir in the grated cheese, olive oil and lemon juice and season to taste.

3. Tear the mozzarella into small chunks and drain on kitchen paper. Toast the bread slices on both sides and, while they are still warm, rub one cut face lightly with the peeled garlic clove. Spread generously with some of the broad bean pâté and top with the mozzarella pieces. Arrange them on a large serving plate and scatter over the rocket leaves. Drizzle with some of the lemon olive oil, scatter with a few sea salt flakes and serve straight away.

Spelt is an ancient grain that's a bit like wheat. It seems to have come back into fashion recently, which pleases us greatly. It's wholesome, hearty and you can now pick it up from most decent supermarkets.

Apple, celery, fennel & spelt salad with cranberries & pomegranate molasses dressing

SERVES 6

125g spelt grain
or Italian farro

1½ tbsp extra-virgin olive oil

1 tbsp pomegranate molasses

¼ tsp sumac, or to taste

50g walnut halves

a 200g bulb of fennel,
outer leaves removed

2 chunky celery stalks

2 small dessert apples

1½ tbsp roughly chopped
mint leaves

1½ tbsp roughly chopped
fennel herb

2 tbsp roughly chopped
flat-leaf parsley

50g dried cranberries

salt and freshly
ground black pepper

1. Preheat the oven to 200°C/Gas 6. Rinse the spelt well, drain and pop into a pan with 750ml cold water. Bring to the boil, cover and simmer for 45 minutes, or until tender but still with a little bit of a bite. Drain well, tip into a bowl and stir in the oil, pomegranate molasses, sumac, ¼ tsp salt and some black pepper. Leave to cool.

2. Spread the walnuts on a baking tray and roast for 6 minutes. Leave to cool, then break into small pieces.

3. Cut the fennel heart in half and slice widthways very finely with a sharp knife or on a mandolin. Thinly slice the celery. Quarter and core the apples and cut them into 1cm pieces.

4. Stir the chopped herbs into the spelt followed by the fennel, celery, apples, walnuts and cranberries. Season to taste and serve straight away.

Top tip:

If you can't get hold of pomegranate molasses or sumac, use a little clear honey and some freshly squeezed lemon juice in their place.

Choose pears that are ripe but still have a bit of crunch. Those with a pink-yellow blush to them will look lovely in this salad. And the caramelised walnuts are to die for!

Autumn salad with pears, pomegranate seeds, blue cheese & caramelised walnuts

SERVES 4-6

2 ripe but firm dessert pears

1 tbsp lemon juice

2 small heads green chicory, broken into separate leaves

2 small heads red chicory, broken into separate leaves

40g watercress sprigs

50g radicchio leaves (optional)

100g de-rinded blue cheese, such as Devon Blue, Beenleigh Blue or Colston Bassett, thinly sliced

the seeds from ½ pomegranate

FOR THE CARAMELISED WALNUTS:

100g walnut halves

2 tbsp clear honey

FOR THE DRESSING:

1½ tbsp red wine vinegar

1 tsp wholegrain mustard

1 tsp clear honey

1 tbsp walnut oil

2 tbsp extra-virgin olive oil

salt and freshly

1. For the caramelised walnuts, preheat the oven to 180°C/Gas 4. Scatter the walnuts over a lined baking tray, drizzle with the honey and roast for 8-10 minutes until toasted and caramelised. Leave to cool, then break into small pieces.

2. For the dressing, whisk together the vinegar, mustard and honey, then gradually whisk in the oils. Season well with some salt and black pepper.

3. Slice the pears away from the core, toss with the lemon juice and set to one side.

4. Toss the salad leaves with 2 tablespoons of the dressing and divide between plates. Tuck the slices of pear and cheese in between the leaves and scatter over the walnuts and pomegranate seeds. Drizzle a little more dressing over and around each plate and serve straight away.

Or you could try...

Apple, pecan & dried cranberry salad. Replace the pears with well-flavoured apples such as Cox's or russets, the walnuts with pecans, use maple syrup instead of honey in the dressing and for the nuts, and dried cranberries instead of the pomegranate seeds. Some very thinly sliced celery adds a nice extra crunch

Beetroot grows pretty much all year round, so it's almost a constant fixture at our tea room. We think it's best roasted with a splash of balsamic – it gives a really deep, slightly caramelised flavour.

Orange-roasted beetroot salad with goats' cheese & dill

SERVES 6-8

1kg small beetroot
(ideally multi-coloured)

grated zest and juice of
1 small orange

2½ tbsp apple balsamic vinegar

5 tbsp extra-virgin olive oil

1 tsp clear honey

2 garlic cloves, crushed

1 tbsp chopped dill,
plus extra to garnish

150g soft rindless
goats' cheese, crumbled

50g toasted walnut pieces
or skinned, halved hazelnuts

25g pumpkin seeds

salt and freshly
ground black pepper

1. Preheat the oven to 190°C/Gas 5. Trim the stalks from the beetroot, peel and cut into bite-sized wedges. Place them in a small roasting tin.

2. Add the orange zest to the beetroot with 2 tablespoons of the juice, 1 tablespoon of the vinegar, 2 tablespoons of olive oil, ½ teaspoon salt and some pepper. Toss together well, cover the tin tightly with foil and roast for 45 minutes–1 hour until just tender. Remove and leave to go cold.

3. Whisk the rest of the vinegar with the honey, then whisk in the remaining oil. Stir in the garlic and season to taste. Spoon the dressing over the beetroot with the 1 tablespoon of chopped dill and mix together well. Transfer to a shallow serving bowl, scatter over the goats' cheese, nuts, pumpkin seeds and extra dill, and serve.

Or how about...?

Roasted beetroot, pomegranate and rocket salad

Roast the beetroot as above but using lemon zest and juice instead of orange. Make a dressing of 1 tbsp pomegranate molasses, 1 tbsp lemon juice, 1 tsp honey, 1 small crushed garlic clove and 3 tbsp extra-virgin olive oil. Season well. Stir through the beetroot with 50g toasted pine nuts, the seeds from 1 pomegranate and 30g rocket leaves.

When we were children, our mum was always urging us to eat our greens, often finding imaginative ways to sneak them into meals. We no longer need such encouragement, especially with delicious recipes like this.

Summer green tabbouleh

SERVES 6

100g medium-grain bulgar wheat

2 tbsp extra-virgin olive oil

200g courgettes,
cut into 1cm dice

150g freshly podded broad beans

75g fine French beans,
topped and tailed and
cut into 1cm pieces

75g freshly shelled peas

1 romaine or little gem
lettuce heart, finely sliced

75g piece cucumber, peeled,
seeds removed and cut into
small dice

the leaves from a small
bunch of fresh mint,
finely shredded

the leaves from a small
bunch of flat-leaf parsley,
coarsely chopped

4 spring onions, trimmed
and thinly sliced

50g toasted pine nuts

1½–2 tbsp lemon juice

salt and freshly
ground black pepper

1. Put the bulgar wheat in a large bowl and cover with plenty of boiling water. Leave to soak for about 10 minutes, or until the wheat is just cooked but still a little al dente. Drain well, then spread it onto a clean tea towel and leave for 15 minutes or so, to remove as much of the excess water as you can.

2. Heat 1½ teaspoons of olive oil in a pan, add the courgette and some seasoning and toss over a high heat for 3 minutes until lightly golden brown and just tender. Spoon onto a plate and leave to cool.

3. Cook the broad beans in boiling salted water for 3 minutes until just tender. Scoop out with a slotted spoon into a colander, run under cold water and leave to cool. Add the French beans to the water and cook for 3 minutes. Add the peas, return to the boil and cook for 1 minute, then drain. Refresh under running cold water, then drain well. Nick the skins of the broad beans with your fingernail and pop the bright green beans out of their skins.

4. Tip the bulgar wheat into a large mixing bowl and stir in the courgette, beans and peas, lettuce, cucumber, chopped herbs, spring onions, pine nuts, lemon juice, remaining olive oil, and plenty of salt to taste. Spoon onto a large serving plate and serve straight away while the lettuce is still crunchy.

Why not try...?

Serving this with some yogurt cheese (see page 14) or feta cheese, crumbled over the top. Or adding a bit of lovely British asparagus when it's in season.

You can use any type of green leaf for this tart, but we favour ruby chard. With its striking red stalks and veins, it's always a talking point with visitors to our organic gardens.

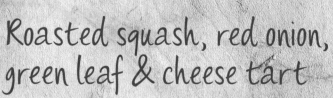

Roasted squash, red onion, green leaf & cheese tart

SERVES 6-8

2 small red onions

375g prepared butternut or other winter squash, cut into 2.5cm pieces

2 tbsp olive oil

300g chard or spinach leaves, large stalks removed and coarsely shredded

225g well-flavoured cheese, crumbled or coarsely grated

3 large free-range eggs

300ml double cream

salt and freshly ground black pepper

FOR THE WHOLEMEAL PASTRY:

150g plain flour

75g stoneground wholemeal flour

65g chilled butter, cut into small pieces

65g chilled lard, cut into small pieces

1. For the pastry, put the flours into a food processor with the butter, lard and $1/2$ teaspoon salt. Whiz together until the mixture looks like fine breadcrumbs, then add 2 tablespoons of cold water and blitz briefly until the mixture comes together in a ball. Turn out onto a lightly floured surface and knead briefly until smooth. Thinly roll out the pastry on the floured surface and use to line a lightly greased 23cm loose-bottomed tart tin 4cm deep. Prick the base here and there with a fork and chill for 20 minutes. Preheat the oven to 200°C/Gas 6.

2. Peel the onions, leaving the root end intact, then slice each one through the root into thin wedges. Put the squash and onion wedges into a roasting tin with the olive oil and some salt and pepper and toss together. Spread out in a layer and roast for 20-30 minutes or until just tender.

3. Line the pastry case with greaseproof paper and fill with a thin layer of baking beans. Bake for 15-20 minutes until the edges are biscuit-coloured. Remove the paper and beans and return to the oven for 5-7 minutes until the base is crisp and golden.

4. Meanwhile, heat a large pan over a medium-high heat, add the chard or spinach leaves and cook for 2-3 minutes until wilted. Tip into a colander and gently press out the excess liquid. Season lightly.

5. Remove the pastry case from the oven and lower the oven temperature to 190°C/Gas 5. Arrange the roasted squash, onion, green leaves and cheese in the pastry case. Beat the eggs and cream with some seasoning, pour over the filling and bake for 30-35 minutes until set and richly golden on top. Serve warm.

These spicy fritters are a bit like Indian pakoras. They're ideal at lunchtime with a salad, as a starter before a curry, or you can make smaller ones and serve them as nibbles with drinks.

Carrot & coriander fritters with green yogurt sauce

SERVES 4 (MAKES 12 LARGE OR 24 SMALL FRITTERS)

25g butter

1 bunch spring onions, trimmed, cleaned and thinly sliced

2 large free-range eggs

80ml whole milk

90g plain flour

½ tsp baking powder

1 tsp ground cumin

¼ tsp turmeric powder

¼ tsp cayenne pepper

350g coarsely grated carrots

25g parmesan, finely grated

15g coriander leaves, chopped

sunflower oil, for shallow frying

salt and freshly ground black pepper

FOR THE GREEN YOGURT SAUCE:

100g wholemilk natural yogurt

1 garlic clove, crushed

¼ tsp caster sugar

¼ tsp salt

15g mint leaves

15g coriander leaves

1 tbsp extra-virgin olive oil

1. For the green yogurt sauce, put all the ingredients into a food processor and blitz until smooth. Spoon into a bowl and chill for 1 hour.

2. Preheat the oven to 110°C/Gas ¼ and line a baking tray with plenty of kitchen paper.

3. Melt the butter in a small pan, add the spring onions and cook for 1 minute until softened. Set aside. Beat the eggs and milk together in a bowl, then sift over the flour, baking powder, cumin, turmeric, cayenne pepper and ¾ teaspoon salt. Whisk together.

4. Pile the grated carrot in the centre of a clean tea towel and squeeze out the excess liquid. Stir into the batter with the spring onions, parmesan and coriander.

5. Pour 1cm oil into a large, deep frying pan and heat it to 180°C. Drop 4 large or 8 smaller spoonfuls of the batter into the oil and flatten the mixture slightly with the back of a spoon. Fry until crisp and golden brown — 1½ minutes on each side for larger fritters or 1 minute for smaller ones. Lift onto the paper-lined tray and keep warm in the oven while you cook the rest. Serve warm with the green yogurt sauce.

This recipe was inspired by some very good little veggie pies we had at the original Bill's in Lewes. If you'd rather make one big pie, use a 23cm x 4cm loose-bottomed tart tin.

Beetroot, new potato & crème fraîche pies

SERVES 6

25g butter

1 medium onion, chopped

2 garlic cloves, crushed

200g peeled waxy potatoes, cut into 5mm thick slices

120ml whole milk

120g crème fraîche

125g coarsely grated Caerphilly, Cheshire or Lancashire cheese

125g coarsely grated cheddar

250g large beetroot, peeled and coarsely grated

20g bunch chives, chopped

salt and freshly ground black pepper

FOR THE PASTRY:

225g plain flour

65g chilled butter, cut into small pieces

65g chilled lard, cut into small pieces

1. For the pastry, sift the flour and ½ teaspoon salt into a food processor, add the butter and lard and whiz briefly until the mixture looks like fine breadcrumbs. Add 2 tablespoons cold water and blitz until the mixture comes together into a ball. Tip out onto a lightly floured surface and knead briefly until smooth, then divide into 6 pieces. Roll out into 15cm discs and use to line 6 lightly buttered 10cm tart tins, 3cm deep. Prick the bases here and there with a fork and chill for 20 minutes.

2. Preheat the oven to 200°C/Gas 6. Line the pastry cases with foil and fill with baking beans. Place on a baking tray and bake for 15 minutes until the edges are biscuit-coloured. Remove the foil and beans and return the cases to the oven for 5-7 minutes until the bases are crisp and golden. Set aside.

3. For the filling, melt the butter in a large pan, add the onion, cover and cook over a low heat for 10 minutes until soft and lightly browned. Uncover, add the garlic and cook for 1 minute more. Add the potatoes, milk, crème fraîche, ½ teaspoon salt and some black pepper and simmer gently for 15-20 minutes, stirring regularly, until the potatoes are tender. (Watch they don't catch on the base of the pan.)

4. Remove the pan from the heat and stir in 75g of each of the grated cheeses, the beetroot and chives. Season to taste. Spoon the mixture into the pastry cases and sprinkle with the remaining cheese. Bake for 10 minutes until the cheese is melted and bubbling.

We normally make this with a good local cheddar like Keen's or Montgomery's, but a decent supermarket cheese like Tickler will give good results, too. Serve it with a simple salad, or as a side dish for roast chicken or lamb.

Or you could try...? Aubergine gratin. Replace the courgettes and peppers with 2 large aubergines, cut across into 1cm thick slices and griddled until golden as below.

Courgette, tomato & roasted red pepper gratin

SERVES 4

2 small red peppers

15g butter

1 large garlic clove, crushed

600g canned plum tomatoes

1 tbsp fresh oregano leaves

750g large courgettes, cut into 5–6mm thick slices

2 tbsp olive oil

150g coarsely grated cheddar

salt and freshly ground black pepper

1. Preheat the oven to 220°C/Gas 7. Put the red peppers on a baking tray and roast in the oven for 20–25 minutes, turning them once or twice, until the skins are blackened in places and the flesh is soft. Seal them in a plastic bag and leave to cool. Then break them open, discard the stalk and seeds, peel off the skin and tear the flesh into wide strips.

2. Meanwhile, melt the butter in a large, deep frying pan and add the garlic. As soon as it is sizzling, add the plum tomatoes and oregano. Bring to a simmer, breaking up the tomatoes with a wooden spoon, and leave to cook gently for about 40 minutes, stirring, until the sauce is really thick and beginning to stick to the bottom of the pan. Season to taste and spoon half over the base of a large, shallow baking dish.

3. Heat a large ridged griddle until smoking hot, then lower the heat slightly. Toss the courgette slices in the oil and griddle in batches for 2 minutes on each side, seasoning as you go, until marked with dark lines. Set aside on plenty of kitchen paper to drain.

4. Scatter half the griddled courgettes over the tomato sauce, followed by half the red pepper strips and half the grated cheese. Spoon over the remaining tomato then repeat the layers once more, ending with the grated cheese. Bake for 25–30 minutes until lightly golden and bubbling.

We always had great difficulty convincing our children to try cauliflower. That was before we came across this recipe for a jazzed-up cauliflower cheese. Now they complain that we don't make it often enough!

Cauliflower cheese with roasted cherry tomatoes & crispy bacon

SERVES 4

1 small onion, peeled, halved and studded with 6 cloves

500ml whole milk

3 large, fresh bay leaves

½ tsp black peppercorns

40g butter

35g plain flour

1 large, very fresh cauliflower, weighing about 1.5kg, core removed, cut into large florets

200g mature cheddar, coarsely grated, plus more for the top

3 tbsp double cream

2 tsp English mustard

200g large, vine-ripened cherry tomatoes

1 tsp olive oil

12 rashers rindless, smoked streaky bacon

salt and freshly ground white pepper

hot buttered wholemeal toast, to serve

1. Pop the studded onion halves into a pan with the milk, bay leaves and peppercorns. Bring to the boil, then remove from the heat and set aside for 20 minutes.

2. Return the milk to the boil, then strain it, discarding the flavouring ingredients. Melt the butter in a non-stick pan, add the flour and cook over a medium heat for 1 minute. Remove from the heat, beat in the hot milk, then return to the boil, stirring. Simmer gently for 5 minutes, stirring occasionally.

3. Meanwhile, preheat the grill to high. Drop the cauliflower into a large pan of boiling water and cook for 7-8 minutes until tender. Drain really well.

4. Remove the sauce from the heat and stir in 150g of the cheese together with the cream, mustard and seasoning to taste. Toss the cherry tomatoes with the oil and season. Arrange the cauliflower in a shallow ovenproof dish and pour over the sauce. Scatter over the remaining cheese and the tomatoes. Pop the bacon in a roasting tin, slide both under the grill and cook for 5 minutes, until the tomatoes are soft, the cheese is golden and the bacon is crisp. Serve with toast.

Or how about...?

Macaroni cheese. Cook 200g macaroni in boiling salted water for 8 minutes until just tender, drain thoroughly and stir into the sauce. Spoon into the dish, and top with 3 thickly sliced vine tomatoes. Mix the remaining 50g grated cheese with 25g coarse white breadcrumbs, scatter over the top and bake at 190°C/Gas 5 for 20 minutes until golden and bubbling.

We're not normally huge fans of frozen veg, but with peas we make an exception. They're normally frozen within minutes of being picked, so they're actually far tastier than fresh peas that have been hanging around in the fridge for a while.

Warm lamb salad with a pea, mint & feta cheese dressing

SERVES 6

1 x 2.5kg leg of lamb, butterflied

2 little gem lettuces, broken into leaves, washed and dried

¼ cucumber, halved and thinly sliced

salt and freshly ground black pepper

FOR THE MARINADE:

6 tbsp olive oil

the leaves from 2 rosemary sprigs, finely chopped

the leaves from 2 large thyme sprigs, roughly chopped

3 garlic cloves, crushed

finely grated zest and juice of 1 small lemon

FOR THE PEA, MINT AND FETA CHEESE DRESSING:

3 small shallots, very thinly sliced

2 tbsp red wine vinegar

¼ tsp caster sugar

250g frozen peas

8 tbsp extra-virgin olive oil

the leaves from a 20g bunch fresh mint, chopped, plus extra whole leaves for garnish

200g feta cheese, crumbled

FOR THE GARLIC AND MINT YOGURT:

250g wholemilk natural yogurt

1 garlic clove, crushed

2 tbsp extra-virgin olive oil

2 tbsp finely chopped fresh mint

1. Mix the marinade ingredients together in a large shallow dish with 1 teaspoon each of salt and freshly ground black pepper. Add the lamb and turn it over in the mixture a few times until it is well covered. Cover and leave to marinate for at least 4–6 hours, ideally overnight.

2. To make the dressing, put the sliced shallots into a mixing bowl and stir in the vinegar and sugar. Set aside for at least 30 minutes so that the shallots can soften. Cover the peas with warm water and leave them to thaw, then drain well and set to one side. Preheat the oven to 200°C/Gas 6.

3. Pop a ridged cast iron griddle over a high heat until smoking hot, then lower the heat to medium-low. Lift the lamb out of the marinade, shaking off the excess, then place it on the griddle and cook for 5–7 minutes on each side until well coloured. Transfer to a roasting tin, spoon over any remaining marinade and roast for 20-25 minutes. Transfer the meat to a carving board, cover with foil and leave to rest for 5-10 minutes.

4. Meanwhile, tear the lettuce leaves into smaller pieces and scatter them over the base of a large serving platter along with the sliced cucumber. Mix the yogurt ingredients together and season to taste.

5. Add the oil to the shallots and swirl together. Stir in the peas and mint and season to taste.

6. Carve the lamb across into thin slices and pop it on top of the lettuce. Spoon over the pea and mint dressing, scatter over the feta and sprinkle with a few more small mint leaves. Eat straight away with the garlic and mint yogurt.

Ooh, we do love a good frost. Now, that might sound a bit odd, but when you consider that veg like the wondrous curly kale taste so much sweeter after a frost or two, perhaps we don't seem quite so eccentric. Perhaps.

A hearty kale, white bean & sausage stew

SERVES 4-6

4 tbsp olive oil

100g smoked bacon strips or lardons

1 medium onion, halved and thinly sliced

100g dried white beans, such as butter beans, haricot or cannellini, soaked overnight

the leaves from 1 large fresh thyme sprig

200g really meaty pork sausages

15g butter

1 small carrot, peeled and diced

1 celery stalk, thinly sliced

1 small leek, trimmed, cleaned and thickly sliced

1 garlic clove, crushed

350g floury potatoes, peeled and cut into small chunks

300ml good chicken stock, or gammon stock (see page 114)

125g prepared curly kale leaves (i.e. minus any thick, tough stalks etc.), roughly chopped into wide strips

salt and freshly ground black pepper

1. Heat half the oil in a large saucepan. Add the bacon and fry for a minute or two until lightly golden. Stir in the onion, cover and cook over a low heat for 10 minutes until the onion is soft and very lightly browned. Drain the soaked beans and add them to the pan with the thyme leaves and 500ml cold water. Bring to a simmer, part-cover and cook gently for 45 minutes to 1 hour until tender. Add 1/2 teaspoon salt and simmer for a further 5 minutes. Tip into a colander set over a bowl to collect the liquor. Measure the cooking liquor and make up to 300ml with water if necessary. Set both to one side.

2. Meanwhile, heat 1 tablespoon of oil in a small frying pan. Add the sausages and fry them gently until nicely browned, then pop on a plate. Heat the remaining oil and butter in the cleaned out bean pan. Add the carrot, celery, leek and garlic, cover and cook gently for 5-6 minutes. Uncover, add the potatoes, a pinch of salt, some black pepper, the bean cooking liquor and stock. Bring to the boil, cover and simmer for 10 minutes or until the potatoes are almost soft.

3. Meanwhile, slice the sausages across into 1cm thick slices. Uncover the soup, stir in the kale and simmer for 5 minutes. Add the sausages and cooked beans and simmer for another 2-3 minutes, until the kale is tender and the beans and sausages have heated through. Season to taste and serve.

Or you could try...

Making this soup with fresh British or Spanish chorizo sausage. It imparts a lovely spicy paprika flavour and red hue to the stew.

the farmyard

The aroma of an organic, free-range chicken slow-roasting in the oven is surely one of the greatest gastronomic pleasures. Bettered only, perhaps, by the eating of it. We've been keeping chickens for years here at the farm, and happy years they've been – both for us and the chickens themselves. They've got lots of space to run around, which they certainly seem to enjoy.

If you're ever unsure how fresh an egg is, try popping it in a tumbler of cold water. If it sits on the bottom in the horizontal position, it's very fresh. If it tilts up a bit to a semi-vertical position, it's probably up to a week old. And if it floats vertically, it's stale.

To get the most out of your bird, use the leftover carcass to make a first-rate stock — following the method on page 120.

Organic and free-range chickens get to do lots of the things they enjoy most: grazing, pecking the ground, scratching about… and even a spot of dust bathing.

We add crushed oyster shells to our chicken feed — it helps them to produce eggs with good strong shells.

On the farm, we've always used duck eggs in our baking, but recently we've discovered that they're also rather lovely in a salad. As you can see from Frank's expression, bottom right.

Farmer's salad of fried new potatoes, duck eggs & black pudding

SERVES 4

350g small, floury potatoes

15g butter

7 tbsp olive oil

1 x 225-250g black pudding, skinned and cut into 16 slices

200g thick-cut smoked streaky bacon, cut into short fat strips

1 small garlic clove, finely chopped

2 tbsp sherry vinegar

2 tsp honey

1 tsp wholegrain mustard

1 tbsp good walnut oil

4 free-range duck eggs

200g mixed salad leaves (watercress, dandelions, rocket, baby leaf chard and spinach)

salt and freshly ground black pepper

1. Peel the potatoes, cut them in half lengthways, then across into 7mm thick slices. Drop them into a pan of boiling salted water and cook for 3 minutes or until just tender. Drain well.

2. Heat the butter and 1 tablespoon of the olive oil in a frying pan, add the potato slices and fry until crisp and golden brown on both sides. Season with salt and pepper and transfer to a low oven to keep hot.

3. Add another tablespoon of oil and the black pudding slices to the frying pan and fry for 1 minute on each side. Remove to a plate and keep warm.

4. Pour away all but 1 teaspoon of oil from the pan, add the bacon and fry for about 4 minutes until crisp and golden. Set aside with the black pudding.

5. Add 2 tablespoons of the olive oil to the bacon fat left in the pan with the garlic, sizzle for a few seconds then add the vinegar, honey, mustard and walnut oil and whisk into a dressing. Season to taste and keep warm.

6. Heat the remaining oil in a clean frying pan and fry the duck eggs until they are done to your liking, spooning some of the hot oil over the yolks as they cook. Meanwhile, arrange the salad leaves, fried potatoes, black pudding and bacon on 4 plates and drizzle over the warm dressing. Top with the fried eggs, season them lightly, and serve with fresh bread.

This tart is a like a cross between a traditional quiche lorraine, a soufflé and a British egg and bacon pie. It's best served warm, straight from the oven, while it is still light and fluffy.

Souffléd egg & bacon tart

SERVES 6–8

1 tsp sunflower oil

200g thick cut smoked streaky bacon, cut into short fat strips

50g butter

25g plain flour

175ml whole milk, warmed

100g finely grated hard cheese, such as cheddar or Lincolnshire Poacher

150ml double cream

¼ tsp freshly grated nutmeg

3 medium free-range eggs, separated

salt and freshly ground black pepper

FOR THE PASTRY:

225g plain flour

65g chilled butter, cut into small pieces

65g chilled lard, cut into small pieces

1. For the pastry, put the flour into a food processor with the butter, lard and ½ teaspoon of salt and briefly whiz until the mix looks like fine breadcrumbs. Tip into a mixing bowl and stir in about 2 tablespoons of water until everything comes together in a ball, then turn out onto a lightly floured surface and knead briefly until smooth. Thinly roll out the pastry and use to line a lightly greased 23 x 4cm loose-bottomed tart tin. Prick the base with a fork and chill for 20 minutes.

2. Meanwhile, preheat the oven to 200°C/Gas 6. Line the pastry case with greaseproof paper and fill with a thin layer of baking beans. Slide it onto a baking sheet and bake for 15–20 minutes until the edges of the pastry are biscuit-coloured. Remove the paper and beans and return to the oven for 5–6 minutes until the base is crisp and golden.

3. While the pastry case is cooking, make the filling. Heat the oil in a frying pan over a high heat. Add the bacon and fry briskly until lightly golden. Set aside.

4. Melt the butter in a medium-sized pan, add the flour and cook for 1 minute. Remove from the heat and gradually stir in the warm milk. Return to the heat and bring to the boil, stirring continuously, until smooth. Add the grated cheese and cream and stir together, then add the nutmeg, bacon and some salt and pepper to taste and leave to cool slightly.

5. Remove the tart case from the oven and lower the temperature to 180°C/Gas 4. Stir the egg yolks into the sauce. Put the whites in a large, clean mixing bowl and whisk them into soft peaks, then fold into the sauce. Pour the mix into the case and bake for 30 minutes, covering with a sheet of foil after about 20 minutes, until puffed up, set and golden brown. Serve immediately.

The first time we tried these Scotch eggs they were a complete revelation. Forget the chalky yolks and soggy crumbs of those sad, shop-bought versions. These beauties, with their super-crunchy coating, are a different thing entirely.

Herby Scotch eggs with sage & lemon

MAKES 8

8 large free-range eggs

30g butter

100g finely chopped shallot or onion

finely grated zest of 2 small lemons

½ tsp ground mace

2 tbsp chopped fresh sage

700g good pork sausage meat

sunflower oil, for deep-frying

salt and freshly ground black pepper

FOR THE BREADCRUMB COATING:

50g plain flour, plus extra for dusting

3 large free-range eggs, beaten

150g fresh white breadcrumbs or Japanese panko crumbs

1. Lower the eggs into a pan of boiling water and cook for exactly 7 minutes. Remove from the pan and plunge into cold water to stop them cooking, then peel.

2. Melt the butter in a medium-sized frying pan, add the shallot or onion and fry gently for 5-6 minutes until soft but not browned. Tip into a bowl and leave to cool. Add the lemon zest, mace, sage, sausage meat and some salt and pepper and mix together well. Divide into 8 equal pieces and roll each piece into a ball, using lightly floured hands.

3. Lay a large sheet of clingfilm on the work surface and lightly dust it with flour. Lay a ball of the sausage meat on top, lightly dust with flour then cover with more clingfilm and roll out into approximately a 14cm disc. Wrap the sausage meat around the egg and press the edges together to seal, making sure there are no gaps and cracks. Chill in the fridge for at least 15 minutes.

4. Meanwhile, heat some oil in a deep-fat fryer or large saucepan to 180°C. Roll the Scotch eggs in the flour, knock off the excess then coat in the beaten egg and finally the breadcrumbs, pressing them on to give a good coating. Deep-fry for 8-9 minutes until crisp, richly golden and cooked through. Drain briefly on kitchen paper and serve hot with a crisp mixed salad.

Crunchy parmesan & garlic 'picnic' chicken

Children seem to love anything cooked in crunchy breadcrumbs and we must admit, so do we...

SERVES 8

2 garlic cloves, crushed

2 medium free-range eggs

200g fresh white breadcrumbs

100g butter, melted

100g parmesan, finely grated

4 tbsp chopped curly leaf parsley

16 x 100g free-range chicken drumsticks, skinned

4 tbsp sunflower oil

salt and freshly ground black pepper

1. Preheat the oven to 190°C/Gas 5. Beat the garlic, eggs and ¹/₂ teaspoon salt together in a dish. Mix the breadcrumbs and butter in another dish, then add the Parmesan, parsley, ¹/₂ teaspoon salt and some black pepper. Dip the drumsticks one at a time into the egg mixture and then into the cheesy breadcrumbs, pressing them on well with your hands. Set aside.

2. Heat the oil in a large, non-stick frying pan over a medium heat. Add the drumsticks, 4 at a time, and fry gently for just 2 minutes until nicely golden underneath. Lift them carefully onto a rack placed over a large roasting tin, golden-side down. Transfer to the top shelf of the oven and bake for 30-35 minutes until crisp, golden and cooked through. Serve hot or cold.

Cauliflower, caramelised red onion & Caerphilly cake

SERVES 10-12

1 tbsp dried polenta

2 tbsp olive oil

2 large red onions, peeled leaving the root intact and cut into wedges

700g prepared cauliflower florets (approx. 1 large cauliflower)

150g self-raising flour

½ tsp turmeric powder

1½ tsp fennel seeds, lightly crushed

10 large free-range eggs, beaten

75g butter, melted

150g cheddar, coarsely grated

the leaves from 20g bunch flat-leaf parsley, chopped

200g Caerphilly cheese, crumbled

salt and freshly ground black pepper

1. Preheat the oven to 180°C/Gas 4. Dust a greased and lined 23cm clip-sided round cake tin with the polenta, leaving the excess evenly covering the base.

2. Heat the olive oil in a frying pan, add the onions and cook gently for 15-20 minutes until soft and nicely caramelised.

3. Meanwhile, drop the cauliflower florets into a pan of well-salted boiling water and cook for 8-10 minutes until tender. Drain well and leave to cool slightly.

4. Sift the flour, turmeric and ½ teaspoon salt into a large mixing bowl and stir in the fennel seeds. Make a well in the centre, add the beaten eggs and whisk together until smooth. Stir in the melted butter, cheddar, red onions, cauliflower, parsley, 150g of the Caerphilly and some black pepper to taste.

5. Pour the mixture into the tin and scatter over the rest of the Caerphilly. Bake for 45 minutes until set, covering loosely with foil once nicely browned. Remove from the oven and leave to rest for 15 minutes. Carefully run a knife around the tin's edge, remove the cake and serve warm, cut into wedges.

This recipe for sticky onion and raisin chutney makes enough for about four 350g jars, so you'll have leftovers long after the parfait has been polished off. No bad thing at all: it's delicious with everything from cheese to cold cuts.

Chicken liver & cider brandy parfait with sticky onion & raisin chutney

SERVES 8

75g finely chopped shallots

100ml Madeira

100ml ruby port

3 tbsp Somerset cider brandy

the leaves from 2 thyme sprigs

500g unsalted butter

750g fresh chicken livers, trimmed

2 small garlic cloves, crushed

pinch each of freshly ground nutmeg, cloves, cinnamon and allspice

salt and freshly ground black pepper

small gherkins, radishes and thin slices of toast, to serve

FOR THE STICKY ONION AND RAISIN CHUTNEY:

100g raisins

300ml ruby port

120ml sunflower oil

1.5kg red onions, halved and thinly sliced

100g light muscovado sugar

120ml red wine vinegar

1. For the chutney, put the raisins and port in a pan, bring to the boil, then set aside to soak. Heat the oil in a large pan, add the onions and cook slowly for 30 minutes, stirring, until soft and starting to caramelise. Add the sugar and cook for another 30 minutes, stirring occasionally, until richly browned and caramelised. Add the boozy raisins and vinegar and cook for 30 minutes until quite thick. Season with $^1/_2$ teaspoon salt and some pepper and spoon into hot sterilised jars. Cover with wax discs and seal.

2. For the parfait, preheat the oven to 130°C/Gas $^1/_2$. Put the shallots, Madeira, port, brandy and thyme into a small pan and simmer until syrupy and reduced by about three-quarters. Leave to cool. Meanwhile, melt 350g of the butter and leave to cool slightly.

3. Put the chicken livers, garlic, shallot reduction, spices, $1^1/_2$ teaspoons of salt and plenty of black pepper into a food processor and whiz for 1 minute until very smooth. With the machine still running, add the melted butter and blend for a few more seconds, then rub the mix through a fine sieve into a bowl.

4. Pour the mix into an oiled and paper-lined 23 x 9 x 8cm terrine dish or loaf tin and cover with a strip of buttered paper. Put it into a small roasting tin half-filled with boiling water, cover with foil and cook for 45 minutes or until just set. Remove from the roasting tin and leave to cool, then chill overnight.

5. The next day, gently melt the remaining butter in a small pan, then pour off the clear butter into a small jug, discarding the milky solids that remain. Pour the butter over the parfait and return to the fridge to set. To serve, lift the terrine from its dish and peel away the paper. Slice thinly and serve with the chutney, toast, gherkins and radishes.

Roast chicken is one of our very favourite suppers, but it can be hard to get spot on. That's why we're such fans of pot roasting: it's super-easy and you end up with fabulously juicy breast meat.

Pot-roasted chicken with apples & cider

SERVES 4

1 tbsp sunflower oil

1 x 1.5kg free-range chicken

175g thick-cut streaky bacon, or gammon steak, cut into short chunky strips

1 large onion, chopped

8 small garlic cloves, thinly sliced

2 good fresh rosemary sprigs, roughly chopped

250ml good-quality dry cider

150ml good chicken stock

4 small dessert apples, such as Cox's

50g butter, softened

2 tsp caster sugar

a little freshly grated nutmeg

15g plain flour

2 tbsp double cream

1 tbsp chopped parsley

salt and freshly ground black pepper

1. Preheat the oven to 180°C/Gas 4. Heat the oil in a small flameproof casserole which will fit the chicken snugly. Season the chicken inside and out, put it in the casserole and brown it on all sides. Then lift it onto a plate, add the bacon and fry until crisp and golden brown. Add the onion and cook over a medium heat for about 5 minutes until soft, then add the garlic and rosemary and fry for a further 2-3 minutes.

2. Add the cider and simmer vigorously until it has reduced by about three-quarters. Put the chicken back in the casserole, pour over the stock, cover with foil and pop the lid on. Cook in the oven for 1 hour.

3. While your chicken is cooking, peel, quarter and core the apples and cut into thick wedges. Melt 25g of the butter in a non-stick frying pan, add the apples and fry them for a few minutes until they begin to brown. Turn the slices over, sprinkle over the sugar and nutmeg and continue to fry for 2 minutes until they are just tender and nicely golden. Remove from the heat.

4. When the chicken is cooked, lift it onto a big chopping board, cover it tightly with foil and leave it to rest for 10 minutes. Put the casserole over a medium heat and simmer until the cooking juices are reduced and full of flavour. Mix the remaining butter with the flour, stir into the reduced juices and simmer for a few minutes, stirring, until thickened. Mix in the double cream and season to taste. Stir in the parsley and apples. Carve the chicken and divide it between 4 nice warm plates. Spoon over the sauce and serve.

We adore coq au vin, but when cooking it ourselves here in Somerset, we like to keep the ingredients pretty local. So rather than a burgundy or a beaujolais, we often use a good fruity red from Polgoon Vineyard in Cornwall.

Chicken braised in local red wine with mushrooms & smoky bacon

SERVES 4-6

1 tsp olive oil

200g thick-cut, dry-cured, smoked streaky bacon, cut into short thick strips

1 x 2kg free-range chicken, jointed into 8 pieces

100g butter

1 onion, halved and sliced

1 large carrot, peeled and sliced

1½ celery stalks, sliced

4 garlic cloves, sliced

4 tbsp Somerset cider brandy

1 bottle fruity red wine

approx. 300ml good chicken stock

2 tbsp redcurrant jelly

1 tbsp tomato purée

4 fresh bay leaves

1 large sprig thyme

300g baby carrots, trimmed

300g peeled button onions or small shallots

pinch caster sugar

250g small chestnut mushrooms

25g plain flour

salt and freshly ground black pepper

1. Heat the oil in a flameproof casserole. Add the bacon and fry gently until crisp, then scoop out onto a plate. Season the chicken pieces, add them to the pan and fry until nicely golden on all sides. Set aside.

2. Add 15g butter, the onion, carrot, celery and garlic to the pan and fry until the onion is nicely browned. Return the chicken to the pan and turn up the heat. Pour over the cider brandy, set it alight and wait for the flames to die down, then pour over the red wine and enough stock to cover. Add the redcurrant jelly, tomato purée and herbs, cover and simmer for 1 hour, or until the chicken is very tender.

3. Meanwhile, melt 15g butter in a small pan, add the baby carrots and 2 tablespoons water. Season, cover and cook gently for 6-8 minutes until tender. Heat 20g butter in another pan, add the button onions, a pinch of sugar and some seasoning, cover and fry gently for 10-15 minutes until soft and golden.

4. Lift the cooked chicken pieces out with a slotted spoon onto a plate, cover and keep warm. Strain the cooking liquid and return to the casserole, skimming the excess fat from the surface, then boil rapidly until reduced to about 750ml. Melt 25g of the remaining butter in a pan, add the mushrooms, season and toss over a high heat for 2-3 minutes until lightly browned.

5. Mix the remaining 25g butter with the flour, whisk it into the sauce and simmer for 2-3 minutes until nicely thickened. Return the chicken to the casserole with the bacon and veg. Season to taste, heat through and serve with buttery new potatoes.

To make your own stock, pop the chicken carcass, wing tips and giblets in a pan with an onion, a carrot, some celery, 4 bay leaves, a few peppercorns and a thyme sprig. Cover with water, bring to the boil, then simmer for an hour. Strain and it's ready to go.

When we we were growing up, Mum used to cook her roast chicken in one of those oval enamelled dishes with a lid; it was always so wonderfully moist and tender. If you don't have one, a normal roasting tin and a sheet of foil like this works just fine.

Slow-roasted chicken with thyme, lemon & garlic

SERVES 4-6

1 x 2kg chicken

1 lemon, halved

4 fresh thyme sprigs

4 fresh bay leaves

1 tbsp sunflower oil, plus extra for roasting

the cloves from 1 small head garlic, separated but left unpeeled

450g pork chipolata sausages

250ml good chicken stock

1 tbsp plain flour

12 rashers rindless streaky bacon, rolled

salt and freshly ground black pepper

FOR THE BREAD SAUCE:

1 onion, halved and studded with 15—18 cloves

600ml whole milk

1 fresh bay leaf

8 black peppercorns

100g fresh white breadcrumbs

25g butter

2 tbsp double cream

1. For the bread sauce, put the onion halves, milk, bay and peppercorns in a pan. Bring to the boil, then set aside to infuse. Preheat the oven to 190°C/Gas 5.

2. Pat the chicken dry and season inside and out. Stuff with the lemon, thyme and bay leaves, truss the bird and drizzle with a little oil. Put the garlic cloves in the centre of a roasting dish or tin, pop the chicken on top, and add 2-3mm water to the tin. Cover with a lid or a large sheet of tented foil over the tin sealed well to the edges. Roast for 1¼ hours.

3. Put the chipolatas into a small roasting tray with a little oil. Increase the oven temperature to 220°C/ Gas 7. Uncover the chicken and roast with the sausages for another 15 minutes until the skin is golden and crispy. Place the chicken breast-side down onto a carving board, cover with foil and leave to rest for 15 minutes. Cook the sausages for another 10–15 minutes until golden brown. Bring the milk for the bread sauce back to the boil, then strain. Return it to the pan and stir in the breadcrumbs and the butter. Set aside.

4. Meanwhile, preheat the grill to high. Pour the excess fat from the roasting tin, put the tin over a medium heat and add a splash of stock. Rub the base with a spoon to release all the juices. Stir in the flour, cook for 1 minute, then gradually add the remaining stock, mashing the garlic as you go. Simmer for 5 minutes, then strain into a clean pan, season to taste and keep hot.

5. Grill the bacon rashers for 5 minutes, turning once until crisp. Uncover the chicken and pour any excess juices into the gravy. Reheat the bread sauce, stir in the cream and season to taste. Carve the chicken and serve with the accompaniments and veg of your choice.

Now here's a recipe that could only come from England. Radishes, tomatoes, baby beetroot, spring onions, cucumbers, new potatoes, lettuce: it's like an English garden on a plate.

Warm English chicken salad with tarragon salad cream

SERVES 6

1 x 1.75kg chicken

1 quantity Tarragon & garlic butter (see page 17), softened

4 large, unpeeled garlic cloves, flattened under the blade of a knife

1 tbsp olive oil

500g new potatoes

4 large free-range eggs

the leaves from the centre of 3 soft, round lettuces, separated

6 small, cooked beetroot, peeled and cut into wedges

½ cucumber, peeled, halved and cut across into chunky slices

6 small, ripe, vine-ripened tomatoes, cut into wedges

1 bunch young spring onions, trimmed and cut into 2

1 bunch small radishes, washed, trimmed and halved lengthways

salt and freshly ground black pepper

FOR THE TARRAGON SALAD CREAM:

150g good mayonnaise

½ tsp English mustard

1 tbsp tarragon or white wine vinegar

3 tbsp single cream

1 tbsp chopped tarragon

pinch caster sugar

1. Preheat the oven to 200°C/Gas 6. Flip your chicken onto its breast and, using poultry shears or kitchen scissors, cut along either side of the backbone. Open the chicken out, turn it breast-side up again, then press your hand firmly along the breast bone until it lies flat. Carefully push your fingers between the skin and the flesh, leaving the skin attached only at the end of each leg. Spoon small amounts of the butter evenly under the skin, pushing it into place from the outside. Secure the skin at the neck opening in place with a small, fine trussing skewer.

2. Scatter the flattened garlic cloves down the centre of a lightly oiled roasting tin and place the chicken on top, skin-side up. Brush with oil, season and roast for about 35–40 minutes, or until the juices run clear when the thickest part of the meat is pierced with a skewer. Lift the chicken onto a board, wrap it loosely in foil and leave it to rest for about 15–20 minutes until it is just cool enough to handle.

3. Meanwhile, put the potatoes into a pan of water, bring to the boil and cook until tender. Put the eggs in a pan of simmering water and cook for 8 minutes. Mix the salad cream ingredients together.

4. Drain the potatoes and, when cool enough to handle, cut in half. Peel the eggs and cut into quarters. Pull the chicken meat away from the bones in large chunks. Scatter the lettuce leaves over a large plate and arrange the warm chicken, potatoes, eggs, beetroot, cucumber, tomatoes, spring onions and radishes in among the leaves. Drizzle over some of the salad cream and serve with the remainder in a separate bowl.

As much as we're partial to wild mushrooms
(we do love a forage!), sometimes only a good
old chestnut mushroom will do. And this is
one of those times.

Chicken & mushroom lasagne

SERVES 6-8

9 sheets (about 175g)
dried lasagne pasta

1 tbsp olive oil

30g butter

300g chestnut mushrooms,
wiped clean and thickly sliced

the meat from 1 large roasted
chicken (approx. 600g),
pulled into chunky pieces

50g parmesan, finely grated

FOR THE SAUCE:

1 small onion,
peeled and halved

4 cloves

1 litre whole milk

2 fresh bay leaves

2 fresh thyme sprigs

1 tsp cracked black peppercorns

75g butter

65g plain flour

1½ tsp freshly grated nutmeg

50ml double cream

1. For the sauce, stud the onion halves with the cloves
   and put them into a pan with the milk, bay leaves,
   thyme and peppercorns. Bring to the boil, remove
   from the heat and set aside for at least 20 minutes
   to allow time for the flavours to infuse.

2. Bring a large pan of well-salted water to the boil.
   Return the milk to the boil, then strain through a
   sieve into a jug. Melt the butter in a medium-sized
   pan, add the flour and cook gently for 2-3 minutes
   without colouring. Remove from the heat and gradually
   stir in the hot milk. Return to the boil, stirring
   constantly, and leave to simmer gently over a very
   low heat, stirring occasionally, for 10 minutes.
   Preheat the oven to 200°C/Gas 6.

3. Drop the sheets of lasagne pasta one at a time
   into a pan of boiling salted water, add the oil and
   cook for 12 minutes or until al dente. Drain well,
   run briefly under cold water, then separate and lay
   them out side by side on a large sheet of clingfilm.

4. Stir the nutmeg and cream into the sauce. Melt the
   butter in a frying pan, add the mushrooms and some
   seasoning and fry briskly over a high heat for 3-4
   minutes until all the excess moisture has evaporated.
   Stir them into the sauce with the chicken and some
   seasoning to taste.

5. Lightly butter a 20 x 29cm shallow baking dish and
   line the base with 3 of the cooked lasagne sheets.
   Spoon over one-third of the chicken sauce and cover
   with another layer of the lasagne sheets. Repeat these
   layers once more, then spoon over the remaining sauce
   and sprinkle over the parmesan.

6. Bake for 30-35 minutes, until golden and bubbling.
   Serve with a mixed leaf salad and hot garlic bread.

We have lots of ducks on the farm; they love our little pond. You can make this with wild mallard if you can get your hands on it, but it's just as delicious made with a duck from your local butcher.

Pan-fried duck breasts with redcurrant & orange sauce

SERVES 4

2 large oranges

25g golden caster sugar

2 tbsp red wine vinegar

150ml good chicken or duck stock

1 tbsp redcurrant jelly

1 tbsp lemon juice

1 tbsp orange flavoured liqueur, such as Grand Marnier (optional)

¾ tsp arrowroot

50g fresh redcurrants, stripped off their stalks with a fork

4 x 175-200g duck breasts

salt and freshly ground black pepper

1. Peel the zest from quarter of one orange and cut into long, fine shreds. Drop them into a pan of boiling water, leave for 5 seconds, then drain and refresh under cold water. Drain on kitchen paper. Squeeze the juice from both oranges and measure out 150ml.

2. Put the sugar and red wine vinegar in a small pan over a low heat, stirring once or twice, until the sugar has dissolved. Increase the heat and boil vigorously until the syrup has turned an amber-coloured caramel. Carefully add the stock, redcurrant jelly and orange juice, bring to the boil and leave to simmer until it has reduced by about half. Stir in the lemon juice, and orange liqueur. Mix the arrowroot with 2 tablespoons of cold water, add to the sauce and simmer for 1 minute. Stir in the orange zest, season to taste and keep warm.

3. Lightly score the skin of each duck breast into a diamond pattern, taking care not to cut into the flesh. Season the meat with both salt and pepper and the skin with just salt. Heat a dry, heavy-based frying pan over a high heat. Add the breasts, skin-side down, lower the heat to medium and cook for 4 minutes until the skin is crisp and golden. Turn the breasts over and cook for 5 minutes if you like your duck pink, or a little longer if you prefer it more cooked.

4. Pop the duck breasts onto a board, cover with foil and leave to rest for 5 minutes, then slice them diagonally into long thin slices and lift them onto warmed plates. Stir the redcurrants into the sauce, bring it back to a simmer, then spoon it over the duck. Serve with peas, creamy mash and a few green leaves.

Every Boxing Day our grandmother would roast a goose for the whole family – a wonderful tradition.

Honey-roasted goose with spiced apple sauce & port gravy

SERVES 8

1 x 4.5kg fresh, oven-ready goose, excess fat and giblets removed

1 small bunch fresh sage

3 tbsp clear honey

salt and freshly ground black pepper

FOR THE PORT GRAVY:

1 small onion, roughly chopped

1 carrot, roughly chopped

25g butter

1 tbsp plain flour

150ml ruby port

900ml good chicken stock

FOR THE SPICED APPLE SAUCE:

50g butter

2 Cox's apples, peeled, quartered, cored and roughly chopped

1 large Bramley apple (approx 450g), peeled, quartered, cored and roughly chopped

finely grated zest of ½ small lemon

25g caster sugar

½ tsp freshly grated nutmeg

8 cloves

1. Preheat the oven to 220°C/Gas 7. Season the cavity of the goose with salt and pepper, push in the sage and tie it together with string. Season the skin with salt, place it on a rack over a large roasting tin and roast for 30 minutes. Lower the oven to 180°C/Gas 4. Remove the goose from the oven and pour the fat from the tin into a bowl. Return to the oven and roast for another hour, pouring off more fat after another 30 minutes. Remove from the oven once more, brush the skin with the honey and return to the oven for a final 30 minutes. The goose will be done when the juices run clear when the thickest part of the leg is pierced with a skewer.

2. While the goose is roasting, make the gravy and apple sauce. Heat 1 tablespoon of the reserved goose fat in a medium-sized pan, add the onion and fry until well browned. Add the carrot, allow to brown lightly, then stir in the butter and flour. Gradually add the port and stock and leave to simmer vigorously until well-flavoured and reduced to a good gravy consistency. Strain into a clean pan, season and keep hot.

3. For the apple sauce, melt the butter in a small pan, add both types of apple, lemon zest, sugar and spices, cover and cook gently for 5-10 minutes until the Bramley has reduced to a purée and the Cox's are tender. Season to taste and keep warm.

4. When the goose is cooked, strain any juices from the cavity into the gravy and put it onto a carving board. Cover with foil and leave to rest for 15-20 minutes. Arrange the meat on a large, warmed platter and serve with the apple sauce, gravy and veg of your choice. To carve, slice off the legs, cut them in half at the joint and then slice the meat away from the bones. Slice the breast meat away from the carcass in two whole pieces and then carve each one lengthways into long, thin slices.

the pastures

Someone once told us that the top six
inches of soil supports all life on earth.
(Thinking about it, it might well have
been our school teacher!) Whoever it was,
it really stuck with us and keeping our
soil super-healthy, in a way that's
completely sustainable, has always been
at the heart of everything we do here
at Yeo Valley. Well, we think it makes for
far tastier dairy, not to mention meat...

We like to think of our pastures as huge solar panels.

With the sun's help, clover-rich grass grabs nitrogen from the air and fixes it into the soil.

This super-healthy soil then repays us by growing top-notch grass for our animals to graze on.

Some salt beef needs a long soak before you cook it, so always check with your butcher. And don't throw away the precious cooking liquor, this makes a wonderful stock for a soup or stew.

Hot salt beef sandwich on rye with mustard & gherkin tartare & leaves

SERVES 8

approx. 2kg piece unrolled salted brisket

2 carrots, halved

4 celery stalks, quartered

1 large onion, quartered

small bunch parsley

small bunch thyme sprigs

6 bay leaves

8 cloves

1 tbsp cracked black peppercorns

FOR THE MUSTARD AND GHERKIN TARTARE SAUCE:

150g thick homemade mayonnaise

50g Greek-style yogurt

1 tbsp English mustard

50g finely chopped gherkins

25g capers, drained well and chopped

1 tbsp chopped curly leaf parsley

½ tsp cider vinegar

TO SERVE:

1 good rye loaf, thinly sliced and buttered

salad leaves and sliced cucumber or pickled cucumbers

1. If necessary, soak the salt beef in cold water for 24 hours, changing the water regularly. Otherwise, simply rinse it well under running cold water.

2. Put the beef into a really large pan or flameproof casserole and cover by at least 8cm with cold water. Bring to the boil then reduce the heat to a very gentle simmer. The water should not be moving, with only a few tiny bubbles appearing from the base of the pan. (This is very important if you want to achieve meltingly tender beef.) Simmer for 20 minutes, then skim off the scum from the surface and add the rest of the ingredients. Simmer for another 2 hours 40 minutes, keeping the temperature consistent and topping up the water from a boiling kettle so that the beef remains well covered at all times. The beef is cooked when a fork will slide into the meat with little or no resistance. Remove from the heat and leave the beef to rest in the hot liquid for 30 minutes.

3. Meanwhile, mix together the tartare sauce ingredients. Spread a little of the tartare sauce on the buttered bread. Lift the salt beef onto a board and slice it thinly across the grain. Put some sliced cucumber, lettuce leaves and hot salt beef onto half the bread slices. Place the remaining slices on top. Press down on each sandwich lightly, cut in half and serve.

Our farm is just a stone's throw from the mighty Butcombe Brewery. If you can't get hold of their beer, any good brown ale or stout will do the job brilliantly.

Braised steak in ale with a herby cobbler topping

SERVES 6

1kg chuck steak, cut into 4cm chunks

5 tbsp sunflower oil

200g smoked bacon lardons

500ml good beef stock

25g butter

250g small chestnut or thickly sliced field mushrooms

2 medium onions, halved and thinly sliced

1 tsp white sugar

3 garlic cloves, crushed

20g plain flour

500ml brown ale or stout

the leaves from 3 large thyme sprigs

4 fresh bay leaves

3 tbsp Worcestershire sauce

salt and freshly ground black pepper

FOR THE HERBY COBBLER TOPPING:

165g plain flour

1 tbsp baking powder

90g chilled butter, cut into pieces

1 tbsp thyme leaves

1 tbsp chopped curly leaf parsley

50g finely grated cheddar

1 medium free-range egg

2 tbsp soured cream, double cream or wholemilk natural yogurt

approx. 100ml whole milk

1. Toss the beef with plenty of seasoning. Heat 3 tablespoons of the oil in a flameproof casserole, add the bacon and fry briskly until golden. Remove with a slotted spoon to a plate. Add the beef pieces in batches and brown well over a medium-high heat. Spoon onto a plate.

2. Add half the stock to the pan and rub the base to release all the caramelised juices, then tip back into the rest of the stock. Add half the butter and the mushrooms to the casserole and fry briskly for 1-2 minutes, then set them aside with the beef. Add the remaining oil and butter to the pan with the onions and sugar and fry them for about 15-20 minutes, stirring frequently, until richly caramelised. Add the garlic and cook for 1 minute.

3. Stir in the flour, followed by the ale, stock, thyme, bay and Worcestershire sauce and bring to the boil, stirring. Return the beef, bacon and mushrooms to the pan, season and simmer for 1½-2 hours, stirring occasionally, until the beef is tender and the sauce has reduced and thickened. Remove the bay leaves and leave to cool slightly, then spoon into a shallow ovenproof dish. Preheat the oven to 180°C/Gas 4.

4. For the topping, sift the flour, baking powder and ½ teaspoon salt into a bowl, add the butter and rub together until the mix resembles fine breadcrumbs. Stir in the herbs and cheese. Break the egg into a measuring jug, add the cream and make up to 180ml with milk. Stir into the dry ingredients, then spoon into separate mounds around the edge of the dish. Bake for 35-40 minutes until the cobbles are puffed up, golden and cooked through.

As our mum Mary always says, fat means flavour. So when shopping for a piece of beef, make sure you find one with a good marbling of fat. Your guests will repay you with clean plates.

Weigh your beef and calculate the cooking times. Allow 15 minutes per 500g for medium-rare beef.

Roast rib of beef with a mustard flour crust

SERVES 8

1 onion, halved and thickly sliced

4 carrots, peeled and thickly sliced on the diagonal

1 x 2-bone 3kg rib of beef, chined but not trimmed

a little sunflower oil

2 tbsp plain flour

2 tsp English mustard powder

2 tsp freshly ground black pepper

salt and freshly ground black pepper

FOR THE YORKSHIRE PUDDINGS:

225g plain flour

1/2 tsp salt

4 medium free-range eggs

300ml whole milk

beef dripping or lard, if necessary

FOR THE GRAVY:

25g plain flour

600ml good beef stock

100ml red wine if you wish, or more beef stock

1. Preheat the oven to 230°C/Gas 8. Spread the onion and carrots over the centre of a large roasting tin. Rub the joint with a little oil, season the cut faces with salt and pepper and then score the fat in a diamond pattern with a small, sharp knife. Mix the flour, mustard, pepper and 1/2 teaspoon of salt together and pat the mix firmly onto the fat. Sit the joint on top of the veg and roast in the oven for 20 minutes. Lower the oven to 170°C/Gas 3 and continue to roast the beef for a further 1 hour 10 minutes.

2. Meanwhile, make the Yorkshire batter. Sift the flour and salt into a bowl, make a well in the centre, add the eggs, milk and 150ml water and beat together to make a smooth batter. Set aside for 30 minutes.

3. Transfer the beef to a board, cover with foil and leave to rest for 30 minutes. Increase the oven to 220°C/Gas 7. Pour the excess fat from the tin into a bowl and make up to 2 tablespoons with melted beef dripping or lard if necessary. Spoon 1/2 teaspoon of this fat into each compartment of a 12-muffin baking tray and heat in the oven until smoking hot, then remove carefully and fill each three-quarters full with the batter. Return to the oven and cook for 25-30 minutes until the Yorkshires are puffed up, crisp and golden.

4. Meanwhile, make the gravy. Place the beef tin directly over a medium heat and when it is sizzling hot, stir in the flour. Add a bit of the stock, scraping the tin's base to release all the cooking juices, then gradually add the remaining stock and the wine if using. Bring to the boil, then simmer until reduced and well-flavoured. Strain, season to taste and keep hot.

5. Uncover the beef, pouring any excess juices from the board into the gravy. Carve into thin slices and serve with the puds and gravy.

This is our version of a cottage pie, but made with all the flavours of a proper beef stew. Use good minced beef with at least 10% fat and don't be shy with the Worcestershire sauce.

Beef & barley cottage pie

SERVES 6

100g pearl barley

600ml good beef stock

3 tbsp sunflower oil

150g streaky bacon,
finely chopped

1 large onion,
finely chopped

350g carrots, peeled
and finely diced

1 large celery stalk,
finely chopped

2 garlic cloves, crushed

1.25kg good minced beef

1 tbsp thyme leaves

3 tbsp Worcestershire sauce

1 tbsp tomato purée

2 tsp English mustard

150ml red wine

salt and freshly
ground black pepper

FOR THE POTATO TOPPING:

1.75kg floury potatoes,
peeled and cut into chunks

75g butter

4-5 tbsp soured cream
or crème fraîche

a little freshly grated nutmeg

1. Put the pearl barley, stock and ¼ teaspoon of salt into a small pan and bring to the boil. Cover and simmer for 25 minutes until tender.

2. Meanwhile, heat the oil in a large pan, add the bacon and fry briskly until lightly golden. Add the onion, cover and cook over a medium heat for 5 minutes. Add the carrots, celery and garlic, re-cover and cook for a further 5 minutes until the veg are soft and lightly browned.

3. Add the minced beef, turn up the heat to high and cook for 3-4 minutes, breaking up the meat with a spoon as it browns. Add the thyme, Worcestershire sauce, tomato purée, mustard, wine, cooked pearl barley and stock and simmer for 25-30 minutes until the liquid has reduced and the mixture has thickened. Preheat the oven to 200°C/Gas 6.

4. Meanwhile, put the potatoes into a pan of salted water, bring to the boil and simmer for 15-20 minutes until tender. Drain well, then return to the pan and mash until smooth (or pass them through a potato ricer). Stir in the butter and soured cream and season to taste with nutmeg, salt and pepper.

5. Season the beef mix to taste and spoon it into a large ovenproof dish. Spoon the mash over the top, spread out evenly and then rough up a little with a fork. Bake for 35-40 minutes until bubbling hot and golden brown.

Slow-roasted pork with butter-roasted apples, lemony carrots & cider gravy

SERVES 6-8

2 tsp coarsely crushed
black peppercorns

1 tbsp chopped rosemary

1 tbsp chopped thyme leaves

1 tbsp chopped sage leaves

3 large garlic cloves, crushed

1 tbsp sea salt flakes,
plus extra for sprinkling

2 tbsp olive oil, plus extra
for rubbing

1 x 2.5kg thick, boned out
piece of pork belly, skin
scored with a Stanley knife
at 1cm intervals

2 large onions, sliced

1 tbsp plain flour

150ml dry cider

150ml good chicken stock

FOR THE BUTTER-ROASTED APPLES:

50g butter

8 small dessert apples,
such as Cox's, peeled,
cored and cut into quarters

4 tsp caster sugar

1/4 tsp freshly grated nutmeg

1/4 tsp ground cinnamon

FOR THE LEMONY CARROTS:

750g carrots, peeled and
cut into small triangular chunks

25g butter

1 tbsp caster sugar

1 tbsp lemon juice

1 tbsp chopped parsley

1. Mix the peppercorns, chopped herbs, garlic, salt and oil together into a paste and rub into the meaty underside of the pork. Set aside uncovered for 1 hour.

2. Preheat the oven to 230°C/Gas 8. Spread the onions over the base of a large roasting tin and rest a rack over the tin. Put the pork skin-side up on top, rub the skin with oil and sprinkle with salt. Pour 1cm of water into the tin, add to the oven and cook for 10 minutes, then lower the oven to 170°C/Gas 3 and roast for 2½ hours, adding a little more water if necessary so that the onions don't burn.

3. For the apples, melt the butter in a frying pan, add the apples and fry over a high heat, turning occasionally, until nicely golden. Add the sugar and spices, season and toss together well, then tip into a roasting tin and roast in the oven for 15 minutes.

4. Remove the pork from the oven and raise the temperature back up to 230°C/Gas 8. Put the onion tin to one side. Pop the pork back in the oven and roast for 15-20 minutes until the skin is crisp.

5. Cook the carrots in a pan of boiling salted water until just tender, then drain. Return to the pan with the butter, sugar, lemon juice, ½ teaspoon of salt and some pepper and toss over a medium heat for 2-3 minutes until well coated, then add the parsley.

6. Leave the pork to rest on a board for 10 minutes. Spoon the excess fat out from the onion tin, then place it over a high heat. Stir in the flour, then the cider and stock and simmer until reduced and well-flavoured. Strain and keep warm.

7. Carve the pork meat-side up into slices through the crackling. Serve with the apples, carrots and gravy.

We make our own cider, and rather a lot of it.
As much as we love drinking the stuff, it's always nice
to save some for cooking. A big piece of gammon poached
in West Country cider really is a thing to behold.

Marmalade-glazed gammon
with chunky potato gratin

**SERVES 8, PLUS PLENTY
FOR CUTTING COLD**

1 x 4kg piece boned
and rolled middle gammon

at least 3 litres dry,
inexpensive cider

2 large carrots,
peeled and quartered

2 large onions,
peeled and halved

2 large celery stalks,
quartered

12 cloves

2 tsp crushed coriander seeds

1 tsp cracked black peppercorns

a large sprig of fresh bay leaves

salt and freshly
ground black pepper

FOR THE SPICED MARMALADE GLAZE:

8 tbsp fine-cut marmalade

6 tbsp demerara sugar

¼ tsp ground cloves

approx. 40 whole cloves

FOR THE CHUNKY POTATO GRATIN:

600ml whole milk

600ml double cream

a little freshly grated nutmeg

2kg small, floury potatoes,
peeled and cut into 5-6mm slices

200g grated cheddar

1. Cover the gammon in plenty of cold water and leave
it to soak for 24 hours, changing the water every now
and then. To check it's ready, cut off a small piece of
meat, cook it in simmering water for a few minutes then
taste it. If it's still very salty, give it longer.

2. Put an upturned plate into a large, deep pan, add the
gammon and cover it by at least 3cm with cold water.
Bring slowly to the boil, then drain, add the cider
and top up with water if necessary. Return to the boil,
add the veg, cloves, coriander seeds, peppercorns and
bay leaves, lower the heat until the water is at a
slight tremble and cook for 1½ hours. Check the gammon
regularly towards the end of the cooking time — it's
ready when a skewer slides easily into the joint's
centre and is hot to the touch once removed. Set aside
and leave the gammon in the liquid until cool enough to
handle, then lift it out, remove the string and carefully
peel away the skin without pulling away any fat.

3. For the gratin, heat the milk and cream in a
large saucepan, add the nutmeg and season to taste.
Bring to the boil, stir in the potatoes and simmer
gently for about 10 minutes, turning occasionally,
until just tender. Tip them into two 2.25 litre
buttered shallow baking dishes, shake level and
cover with the cheese.

4. Preheat the oven to 220°C/Gas 7. Lightly score the
gammon fat into diamonds with a sharp knife, then
place in a foil-lined roasting tin. Mix the marmalade,
sugar and cloves and spread thickly over the gammon,
pushing a clove into the centre of each diamond.
Roast for 20 minutes or until the fat is a deep golden
brown. Leave to rest for 20-30 minutes. Lower the oven
temperature to 180°C/Gas 4, slide the gratins into the
oven and bake for 30 minutes until golden and bubbling.
Carve and serve the ham with the gratin and a salad.

We'd recommend seeking out proper big chops for this recipe. They're much more likely to stay nice and juicy than the sad, thin ones you so often see around.

Sweet 'n' smoky pork chops with cabbage & mash

SERVES 4

4 large pork chops on the bone, cut 2.5–3cm thick, and weighing about 400g each

2 garlic cloves

1½ tsp sweet smoked paprika

3 tbsp olive oil

2 tbsp cider vinegar

3 tbsp clear honey or maple syrup

salt and freshly ground black pepper

FOR THE CELERIAC MASH:

600g celeriac, peeled and cut into chunks

300g floury potatoes, peeled and cut into chunks

25g butter

FOR THE BUTTERED CARAWAY AND GARLIC CABBAGE:

1 pointed cabbage, weighing about 750g

25g butter

1 tsp caraway seeds

2 garlic cloves, crushed

1. Slice the rind from each pork chop, leaving behind all the fat, and lightly score the meaty surface on each side with a sharp knife. Flatten the garlic cloves under the blade of a knife, sprinkle with ½ teaspoon of salt and crush them into a paste. Mix with the paprika, olive oil, vinegar, honey and some black pepper. Rub the mixture over both sides of the chops, cover and leave to marinate for 1–2 hours.

2. Preheat the oven to 220°C/Gas 7. Heat a large frying pan over a medium heat. Lift the chops out of the marinade and, using tongs, hold them one at a time on their sides, searing the fatty edge until crisp and golden. Then fry the chops for 2 minutes on each side until lightly browned. Transfer them to a lightly oiled roasting tin, pour over any leftover marinade and roast them for 20 minutes until cooked through, but still juicy in the centre.

3. While the chops are roasting, boil the celeriac and potatoes in well-salted water until tender — about 15–20 minutes. Drain well, return to the pan and mash until smooth. Stir in the butter and season to taste.

4. Meanwhile, shred the cabbage into 1cm wide strips, discarding the core. Drop it into a large pan of boiling salted water, cook for 3 minutes, then drain. Melt the butter in a large pan, add the caraway seeds and garlic and as soon as they start to sizzle, add the cabbage and toss over a high heat for 1 minute until just cooked, but still slightly crunchy. Serve with the pork chops and celeriac mash.

This is a firm favourite with all our family, from the little ones right through to the oldies. The meatballs and the sauce freeze beautifully, so why not double the quantities and save half for a rainy day?

Or you could try...
Cheesy Italian polpetti meatballs
Use all minced beef (omitting the pork and bacon) and add 75g finely grated parmesan to the mix.

Smoky bacon meatballs with pappardelle pasta

SERVES 4

400–500g dried
pappardelle pasta

salt and freshly
ground black pepper

FOR THE MEATBALLS:

4 tbsp olive oil

1 medium onion, finely chopped

2 garlic cloves, crushed

225g dry-cured,
smoked streaky bacon

500g good minced beef

250g good minced pork

finely grated zest of
1 small lemon

75g fresh white breadcrumbs

20g fresh oregano leaves

1 medium free-range egg, beaten

FOR THE TOMATO SAUCE:

1 tbsp olive oil

15g butter

1 medium onion, finely chopped

2 garlic cloves, crushed

1 red pepper, stalk and seeds
removed and flesh finely chopped

½ deseeded and chopped
red chilli (optional)

200g canned chopped tomatoes

350g tomato passata

1 tbsp apple balsamic vinegar

1 tsp caster sugar

a large handful of basil leaves

1. For the meatballs, heat 2 tablespoons of olive oil in a small pan, add the onion and garlic, cover and cook over a low heat for 10 minutes until soft. Tip into a large mixing bowl and leave to cool slightly.

2. For the sauce, heat the oil and butter in a large saucepan or flameproof casserole over a low heat. Stir in the onion, garlic, pepper and chilli if using, cover and cook gently for 10 minutes until softened. Uncover, add the chopped tomatoes, passata, apple balsamic, sugar, ½ teaspoon of salt and some black pepper and bring to a simmer.

3. Put the bacon into a food processor and pulse until finely chopped. Add to the mixing bowl with the minced beef, pork, lemon zest, breadcrumbs, oregano, egg, ½ teaspoon salt and plenty of black pepper and mix together well with your hands. Shape the mixture into walnut-sized balls.

4. Heat the remaining 2 tablespoons of olive oil in a large, non-stick frying pan. Add the meatballs, a few at a time, and brown them all over, then drop them into the simmering sauce. When all the meatballs have been added, part-cover the pan and simmer gently for 20 minutes, stirring gently now and then so as not to break up the meatballs.

5. Meanwhile, bring a large pan of well-salted water to the boil. When the meatballs are ready, add the pappardelle and cook for about 12 minutes, or until tender but still a little al dente. Roughly chop the basil and stir into the meatballs. Serve with the pasta.

You can make this with spring lamb, but we think it's worth waiting until the summer, when the lambs have had plenty of time to feed on fresh pasture. They give a far richer flavour with a little more age on their side.

Roast leg of lamb with rosemary & garlic 'pesto'

SERVES 6

1 x 2.25kg lamb leg

1.5kg floury potatoes, peeled

8 garlic cloves,
peeled and halved

8 x 5cm sprigs rosemary

3 tbsp olive oil

2 tbsp lemon juice

6-8 tbsp good chicken stock

salt and freshly
ground black pepper

FOR THE ROSEMARY AND GARLIC PESTO:

3 garlic cloves, peeled

Sea salt flakes

the leaves from 3 bushy 15cm
rosemary sprigs, finely chopped

finely grated zest of
½ small lemon

4-5 tsp olive oil

1. Preheat the oven to 230°C/Gas 8. Using a small, sharp knife, make little 2.5cm deep slits all over the lamb leg, about 5cm apart.

2. For the pesto, crush the garlic cloves on a chopping board with the blade of a chef's knife, then sprinkle with some salt and crush into a smooth paste. Mix with the chopped rosemary, lemon zest, some black pepper and enough oil to make a paste. Push some of the paste into each slit, then rub the leg with the rest and season. Set aside at a cool room temperature for as long as you like. The longer you leave it, the more time the flavours will have to infuse the meat.

3. Cut the potatoes into roughly 2.5cm pieces. Put them into a large roasting tin with the halved garlic cloves, rosemary sprigs, olive oil, 1 teaspoon of salt and some pepper, toss together well then spread out in an even layer.

4. Place a rack over the tin and put the lamb on top. Put it into the oven and roast for 15 minutes, then lower the oven temperature to 200°C/Gas 6 and roast for a further 30 minutes.

5. Remove the tin from the oven and carefully lift the rack of lamb to one side. Loosen the potatoes from the base of the tin, sprinkle over the lemon juice and chicken stock, and replace the rack of lamb. Return it to the oven to cook for a final 35 minutes.

6. Remove the lamb from the oven, lift the meat onto a carving board, cover with a sheet of foil and leave to rest for 15 minutes. Return the tin of potatoes to a low oven to keep hot. Carve the lamb into slices and serve with the rosemary and lemon potatoes.

Local farmers plough for victory at the 154th annual Mendip Ploughing Match, held right here on our farm. It really was a fantastic day, not least because of the obligatory ploughman's lunch followed by a spot of cider drinking.

We've always been big offal fans, but we know that some people aren't too keen. If you're one of them, this could be the recipe to convert you. It's certainly worked on guests of ours!

Griddled lamb chops with devilled kidneys

SERVES 4

8 lamb's kidneys

20g butter, melted

¼ tsp cayenne pepper

1 tsp English mustard

½ tsp Worcestershire sauce

1 tsp lemon juice

1 tbsp olive oil

8 loin lamb chops

1 tbsp chopped parsley

salt and freshly ground black pepper

FOR THE GRILLED TOMATOES:

6 vine-ripened tomatoes, halved

2 tsp chopped thyme

15g finely chopped pitted black olives

1 small garlic clove, chopped

20g butter

1. Preheat the grill to high. Put the tomato halves side by side in a shallow ovenproof dish and sprinkle over the thyme, olives, garlic and some seasoning. Dot each one with a little of the butter.

2. Cut the lamb's kidneys in half and snip out the cores with scissors. Toss with some seasoning. Mix the melted butter with the cayenne, mustard, Worcestershire sauce and lemon juice. Heat a large, ridged cast iron griddle over a high heat until smoking hot, then lower the heat to medium-high.

3. Put the tomatoes under the grill and cook for 8 minutes until tender. Meanwhile, brush the chops on both sides with a little oil and season well. Put them onto the griddle and cook for about 4 minutes on each side, until nicely browned on the outside but still pink and juicy in the centre. Stand them on their fatty edges and cook for 1 minute more. Lift onto a plate, cover with foil and leave to rest for 2-3 minutes.

4. When the chops are nearly cooked, heat 1 teaspoon oil in a frying pan, add the kidneys and cook over a high heat for 4 minutes, turning them over halfway through, until firm and lightly browned on the outside but still slightly pink in the centre. Add the butter mixture and chopped parsley and toss together well over the heat for 30 seconds, but no longer. Serve with the chops and grilled tomatoes.

Most people love a good curry and we're no exception. We'd recommend cooking this one a day in advance and reheating it – the flavours get deeper as they get to know each other.

Our favourite Sumatran lamb curry

SERVES 6

500g onions

100g ghee or clarified butter

1 x 1.5kg boned lamb shoulder

1 tbsp cumin seeds

1 tbsp coriander seeds

½ tsp cardamom seeds (not pods)

1 tbsp sweet paprika

1½ tsp cayenne pepper

1½ tsp turmeric powder

½ tsp ground cinnamon

5 large garlic cloves

50g piece peeled root ginger, roughly chopped

1-2 large red chillies, deseeded

1 large red pepper, seeded and roughly chopped

400ml coconut milk

1 tbsp tamarind paste

freshly chopped coriander, to garnish

salt and freshly ground black pepper

FOR THE CUCUMBER AND MINT RAITA:

175g piece cucumber

125g wholemilk or Greek-style natural yogurt

1 tsp mint jelly, warmed

1 tbsp chopped fresh mint

1. Thinly slice half the onions. Heat the ghee in a large, flameproof casserole, add the sliced onions and cook over a medium heat, stirring for 15 minutes until they are richly golden brown. Meanwhile, trim all the skin and excess fat from the lamb and cut the meat into 4cm chunks.

2. Put all the spices into a spice grinder (we have a coffee bean grinder reserved just for spices) or a pestle and mortar and grind them into a fine powder. Roughly chop the rest of the onions and put them into a liquidiser with the garlic, ginger, chillies, red pepper, spices, 1 teaspoon of salt and 6-8 tablespoons of cold water. Blend to a smooth paste, stopping and stirring the contents now and then to get the mixture moving if necessary. Add the paste to the fried onions and cook for 5 minutes more, stirring frequently.

3. Stir the coconut milk, tamarind paste and lamb into the pan, cover and simmer gently for 20 minutes. Uncover and continue to simmer for 1¼ hours, until the meat is tender and the sauce is thick. Adjust the seasoning to taste.

4. For the raita, peel the cucumber, halve it lengthways and scoop out the seeds. Finely dice the flesh, toss it with ½ teaspoon of salt and leave it in a sieve to drain for 20 minutes. Dry it well on kitchen paper and mix with the remaining ingredients and a little more salt to taste. Season the curry to taste, scatter over a little chopped coriander and serve with some steamed rice and the cucumber raita.

the woods, hedgerows, fields & streams

We're incredibly lucky to have a lovely chap called Les Davies (MBE!) as our education officer.

He takes groups on tours of the farm and local woodlands. What he doesn't know about the Mendips isn't worth knowing!

Les's foraging top 10

wild garlic
field mushrooms
wild fennel
horseradish
crab apples
blackberries
elderberries
elderflowers
wild plums
damsons

We believe that animals who lead healthy, happy lives make for better eating, which is why we love all things game. All that flying or running about in the wild means the muscles can develop naturally, so game is often both lean and extremely tasty. Slow cooking helps make it lovely and tender.

Remember to give your foraged fruits a good once-over for insects before you use them. Especially when cooking for vegetarians.

One of the best things about living and working in the valley is the wonderful food that surrounds us – and we don't just mean yogurt. The woodlands, hedgerows, fields and streams are abundant with everything from fish and game to berries and mushrooms... not to mention herbs. If you agree, why not put your wellies on and see what you can find?

Wild garlic, with its large, glossy green leaves, has to be one of our favourite things to forage for. Next time you spy bluebells, have a closer look, as there's often wild garlic nearby. If you're uncertain, just follow your nose!

Spinach, wild garlic & filo pie

SERVES 4

250g butter

300g feta cheese

100g ricotta cheese

50g parmesan or pecorino, finely grated

5 large eggs

50g fresh white breadcrumbs

½ tsp freshly grated nutmeg

4 tbsp extra-virgin olive oil

375g fresh filo pastry, not frozen (approx 14 30 x 38cm sheets)

200g fresh spinach leaves, washed and dried well, tough stalks discarded, cut into 1cm strips

150g wild garlic leaves, washed and dried well, tough stalks discarded and leaves cut into 1cm strips

1 bunch spring onions, trimmed and thinly sliced

salt and freshly ground black pepper

Top tip:

When wild garlic is not in season just use all spinach, and flavour the pie with a 50g bunch of chopped fresh mint or dill.

1. Put the butter into a small pan and leave over a low heat until melted. Pour off the clear butter into a bowl, leaving behind the milky-white solids.

2. Crumble the feta into a large bowl and coarsely mash it with a fork. Add the ricotta, Parmesan, eggs, breadcrumbs, nutmeg, oil, spring onions, ½ teaspoon each of salt and pepper and mix together well.

3. Preheat the oven to 180°C/Gas 4. Lightly butter a 20 x 30cm roasting tin, 5cm deep. Unroll the filo pastry onto the work surface. Set aside 7 sheets for the top and cover with a damp tea towel to prevent them drying out. Working as quickly as you can, brush one pastry sheet with the melted butter and pop it buttered-side down to line the base and sides of the dish, leaving about 5cm of the edges overhanging. Repeat this process with another 6 pastry sheets.

4. Add the shredded spinach and garlic leaves to the egg mix and stir together well. Spoon the mixture into the pastry-lined tin and spread it out evenly.

5. Butter one of the reserved pastry sheets and lay it buttered-side down over the pie, pressing it down well onto the top of the mixture. Repeat with the remaining 6 sheets. Press the overhanging edges together then trim to within 2.5cm of the edge of the dish. Lift them up and tuck them down the sides of the pie.

6. Using a sharp knife, mark the top of the pie into 8 pieces. Sprinkle with a little water and bake for 45 minutes until set in the middle, crisp and richly golden, covering loosely with foil if it starts to brown too quickly. Leave to cool for 15 minutes, then cut into pieces along the marked lines and serve.

Taking the family mushroom hunting really is great fun. But always have an expert on hand, as you do hear horror stories. If you don't have a Les of your own, it might be best to head to your local farm shop or supermarket instead.

Field mushrooms in garlic & parsley butter on granary toast with crispy bacon

SERVES 4

2 fat garlic cloves

the leaves from 1 large thyme sprig

100g soft butter

2 tbsp chopped curly-leaf parsley

12–16 thin-cut rashers rindless streaky bacon or pancetta

4 large or 8 smaller thick slices of fresh granary bread

3 tbsp olive oil

750g flat or closed-cup field mushrooms, wiped clean and thickly sliced

salt and freshly ground black pepper

1. Pop the garlic cloves on a board and flatten them under the blade of a large knife. Roughly chop the thyme leaves alongside them, then scoop them together, sprinkle with ½ teaspoon of salt and crush together with the blade of the knife into a paste. Mix with the soft butter, parsley and some black pepper.

2. Heat a large ridged cast iron griddle over a high heat. Lay the rashers of bacon side by side on the griddle and cook until crisp and golden — about 2 minutes on each side. Remove from the heat and keep hot. Toast the bread.

3. Heat a really large frying pan over a high heat. Add half the olive oil and when it is jumping-hot, add half the mushrooms, season them lightly and fry for just 2 minutes, tossing them until slightly browned but still firm. Add half the garlic butter and toss together briefly until the butter has melted.

4. Quickly put the toast onto warmed plates and pile over the mushrooms and their buttery juices. Top with the bacon and serve. Repeat with the remaining mushrooms for the other 2 portions.

Or you could try...

Baked field mushrooms.
Preheat the oven to 220°C/Gas 7 and put 8 large field mushrooms onto a lightly oiled baking tray. Season lightly with salt and pepper, dot with the garlic and parsley butter and bake for 10 minutes until tender. Squeeze over a few drops of lemon juice and serve with crusty bread.

After a bracing yomp in search of field mushrooms, there's no better way to warm the cockles than with this simple and satisfying soup. Perhaps with some nice sourdough toast for dunking.

Field mushroom soup

SERVES 6-8

30g dried porcini mushrooms

100g butter

2 garlic cloves, crushed

200g chopped shallots or onions

the leaves from 2
large thyme sprigs

750g flat or closed-cup field
mushrooms, wiped clean,
peeled and chopped

the leaves from 20g bunch
curly leaf parsley, chopped

30g plain flour

1.2 litres good chicken
or vegetable stock

150g crème fraîche
or double cream

a little freshly grated nutmeg

salt and freshly
ground black pepper

1. Cover the dried porcini with 150ml boiling water and leave to soak for 20 minutes. Meanwhile, melt 75g of the butter in a large pan, add the garlic, shallots and thyme leaves, cover and cook over a low heat for 10 minutes until soft but not browned.

2. Drain the soaked porcini, reserving the liquid, and finely chop. Add them to the softened shallots with three-quarters of the field mushrooms and fry for 5 minutes until the juices from the mushrooms start to run. Stir in the parsley and then the flour, cook for 1 minute, then gradually stir in the stock and all but the last tablespoon of the mushroom soaking liquid (which might be a bit gritty). Bring to the boil, lower the heat, cover and simmer gently for 15 minutes.

3. Let the soup cool slightly then liquidise in batches until smooth. Stir in the crème fraîche or cream. Melt the remaining butter in the pan, add the rest of the mushrooms, season and fry briskly over a high heat for 2 minutes until they begin to colour. Return the soup to the pan and simmer for 3 minutes. Season with nutmeg, salt and pepper and serve with crusty bread.

Or how about...?

Using wild mushrooms when in season. We like a mix of penny buns (ceps/porcini), hedgehog mushrooms (pied de mouton), yellow legs (winter/grey chanterelles), flower of the wood (chanterelles girolles), horn of plenty (trompette de la mort) and oyster mushrooms. Chop up the chunky ones but leave the little ones whole.

SERVES 10-12

750g un-skinned trout fillets, pin-boned

2 tbsp vodka

100g coarse sea salt

75g granulated or caster sugar

2 tbsp finely crushed white peppercorns

2 tsp finely crushed fennel seeds

50g fennel herb or dill, coarsely chopped

finely grated zest of ½ lemon

thin slices of Scandinavian-style rye bread or pumpernickel, lightly buttered, to serve

FOR THE MUSTARD AND HORSERADISH SAUCE:

2 tsp finely grated horseradish, fresh or from a jar

2 tsp finely grated onion or shallot

1 tsp Dijon mustard

¼ tsp English mustard powder

1 tsp caster sugar

2 tsp white wine vinegar

75g sour cream or crème fraîche

75g wholemilk natural yogurt

salt

Trout & fennel gravlax with mustard & horseradish sauce

1. For the gravlax, line a wide, shallow dish with clingfilm and place half the trout fillets in a single layer, skin-side down in the bottom. Brush them with some of the vodka. Mix the salt with the sugar, peppercorns, fennel seeds, chopped fennel herb or dill and lemon zest and spread over the top of the fillets. Brush the cut face of the remaining trout fillets with the remaining vodka and place flesh-side down on top. Cover with another sheet of clingfilm, then place a board on top and weight them down with a few unopened cans. Refrigerate for 24 hours.

2. To serve, remove the fish from the briny mixture, separate the pairs and place skin side down on a board. Starting at the tail end, slice the fish away from the skin, sharply on the diagonal into thin slices as you would smoked salmon.

3. Mix the ingredients together for the mustard and horseradish sauce. Serve on top of the buttered bread, together with a small spoonful of the sauce.

Hyssop is a little-used herb that goes particularly well with pork, lamb and fish such as trout. If you can't track it down, a mixture of mint and thyme works very well indeed.

Whole baked trout with crunchy bacon & hyssop stuffing

SERVES 4

1 tsp sunflower oil

100g rindless smoked streaky bacon rashers, cut across into thin strips

75g butter

100g crustless white bread, cut into 1cm cubes

1 small onion, finely chopped

100g cleaned and trimmed leek, thinly sliced

2 tsp chopped hyssop or mixed chopped mint and lemon thyme leaves

4 tsp chopped curly leaf parsley

1 medium free-range egg

2 tbsp whole milk

4 x 300g trout

salt and freshly ground black pepper

1. Preheat the oven to 200°C/Gas 6. Heat the oil in a frying pan, add the bacon and fry until crisp and golden. Remove with a slotted spoon to a mixing bowl, leaving behind as much of the bacon fat as you can.

2. Add 25g of the butter to the fat in the pan, leave until melted then add the bread cubes and toss together well. Fry over a medium-high heat for about 5 minutes until crisp and golden. Season lightly with salt and pepper and add to the bowl with the bacon.

3. Add another 25g butter to the pan with the onion and fry gently for 5 minutes until soft and golden, then add the leek and fry, stirring, for 2-3 minutes more. Add to the bowl with the chopped herbs and a little more seasoning, mix together well and leave to cool slightly. Beat the egg with the milk and stir 3 tablespoons of it into the stuffing mixture. Leave to soak for 5 minutes.

4. Melt the remaining butter. Season the gut cavity of each fish with salt and pepper, then spoon a quarter of the stuffing into each fish. Partly seal the opening with a small, fine skewer. Place the trout on a lightly buttered baking tray, brush on both sides with melted butter and season. Bake for 15-20 minutes until just cooked through. The flesh should be firm and opaque and should come away easily from the bones at the thickest part just behind the head. Serve straight away.

You can't beat a proper coarse farmhouse terrine, and this is one of our all-time favourites. Top tip: leaving the terrine to chill for a day or two after weighting it down lets the flavours develop wonderfully.

Or you could try...

Gamey devils on horseback

Shape 10g pieces of the terrine mix into little lozenges, then use them to stuff some soft, stoned prunes. Wrap each in half a stretched rasher of streaky bacon, pop on a baking tray and roast at 200°C/Gas 6 for 12–14 minutes, until golden. Serve hot with drinks.

Coarse game & green peppercorn terrine

SERVES 10-12

25g butter

100g finely chopped shallot or onion

2 fat garlic cloves, crushed

3 tbsp ruby port

3 tbsp Madeira

700g mixed boneless game meat (an equal mixture of pheasant, rabbit and venison), finely diced

250g minced belly pork

the leaves from 2 large thyme sprigs

the leaves from 2 x 15cm rosemary sprigs, finely chopped

6 juniper berries, crushed then finely chopped

½ tsp ground mace or freshly grated nutmeg

1–2 tsp green peppercorns in brine, drained, rinsed and roughly chopped

1 medium free-range egg, beaten

300–350g dry-cured smoked streaky bacon

250g fresh duck or chicken livers, snipped into smaller pieces

salt and freshly ground black pepper

1. Melt the butter in a small pan, add the shallot and garlic, cover and cook gently for about 7 minutes until very soft but not browned. Add the port and Madeira and simmer until thick and syrupy. Leave to cool.

2. Put 200g of the chopped game meat into a food processor and pulse until very finely chopped. Pop into a bowl and add the remaining game meat, pork, thyme, rosemary, juniper, mace, green peppercorns, reduced shallot mix, beaten egg, 1 teaspoon salt and ½ teaspoon black pepper and mix together well with your hands. Chill overnight to let the flavours develop if you wish.

3. Stretch the bacon rashers with the back of a kitchen knife and use to line the base and sides of a 900g terrine dish or loaf tin, overlapping them slightly and leaving the ends overhanging. Press one-third of the terrine mixture into the tin's base and lay over a few pieces of liver. Repeat the layers once more, then finish with a final layer of the terrine mix. Fold the overhanging bacon over the top, sealing any gaps with 2–3 more rashers if needed.

4. Preheat the oven to 170°C/Gas 3. Cover the terrine with a lid or lightly oiled foil, pop it into a small roasting tin and half fill with boiling water. Cook in the oven for 1½ hours or until the juices run clear when pierced with a skewer. Remove the terrine from the roasting tin and leave to stand for 15 minutes.

5. Pop a foil-wrapped piece of cardboard over the top of the terrine, weight it down with a few unopened cans and leave to chill in the fridge overnight. Serve cut into slices with crusty bread, cornichons and chutney.

Roasting pheasants is far easier if you do just hens or just cocks, that way all the birds will take the same time to cook. If you can, buy two brace and pop the spare birds in the freezer for next time.

Roasted pheasant with pearl barley & mushroom risotto

SERVES 4

2 plump, oven-ready pheasants, each weighing about 750-800g, well-washed and any stray feathers removed

2 large thyme sprigs

30g butter

8 rindless rashers dry-cured streaky bacon

200ml fruity vintage cider

1 tbsp crab apple jelly

200ml pheasant, game, beef or roasted chicken stock

50g chilled unsalted butter, cut into small cubes

salt and freshly ground black pepper

FOR THE PEARL BARLEY AND MUSHROOM RISOTTO:

40g dried porcini mushrooms

75g butter

1 medium onion, finely chopped

400ml pheasant, game, beef or roasted chicken stock

300g pearl barley

375g wild or chestnut mushrooms, cleaned and sliced

3 tbsp chopped parsley

1 Soak the porcini in 150ml boiling water for 20-30 minutes. Drain, reserving the liquid, then roughly chop and set aside. Preheat the oven to 220°C/Gas 7.

2. Season the pheasant cavities with salt and pepper and stuff each with a thyme sprig and a knob of butter. Season the outside of the birds and truss them neatly with string, then lay 4 bacon rashers over each bird and pop them into a lightly oiled roasting tin. Roast the birds for 15 minutes, then lower the oven to 180°C/Gas 4 and roast for 15 minutes more, removing the bacon once it is crisp and golden and setting it to one side. The pheasants are cooked when the juices run clear when pierced through the thickest part of the thigh.

4. Meanwhile, for the pearl barley risotto, melt 20g of the butter in a small pan, add the onion and fry gently for 5 minutes until soft and lightly golden. Add the porcini and fry for 2-3 minutes more. Add the stock and the pearl barley, cover and simmer gently for 25-30 minutes until the stock has been absorbed and the barley is tender.

5. Transfer the cooked pheasants to a board breast-side down, cover tightly with foil and leave to rest for 5-10 minutes. Pour any excess fat away from the juices left in the tin, place over a medium heat and add the cider, crab apple jelly and stock. Boil rapidly until reduced to about 100ml. Strain into a pan, return to a simmer and whisk in the chilled butter pieces a few at a time. Season to taste and keep warm.

6. Melt the remaining butter in a frying pan, add the mushrooms and stir-fry for 3-4 minutes. Stir into the pearl barley with the parsley and season to taste. Cut the pheasants in half along the breast and backbone and pop them onto warmed plates. Serve with the pearl barley risotto, gravy and some steamed broccoli.

There's something about getting out there and braving the elements that we really enjoy. Not to mention sitting down to a spot of steadying game pie afterwards.

Mixed game pie with sausage meat-stuffing balls

SERVES 6

2 tbsp sunflower oil

50g butter

1kg mixed boneless game meat (rabbit, pheasant, venison and pigeon), cut into small chunks

200g smoked dry-cured bacon, cut into short chunky strips

1 large onion, chopped

the leaves from 2 thyme sprigs

1 tsp juniper berries, crushed

45g plain flour

600ml game, pheasant, roasted chicken or beef stock

150ml ruby port

1 tbsp redcurrant jelly

4 bay leaves

2 carrots, peeled and diced

2 large celery stalks, sliced

1 tbsp sunflower oil

salt and freshly ground black pepper

FOR THE STUFFING BALLS:

225g pork sausage meat

50g rindless dry-cured streaky bacon rashers, chopped

75g cooked and peeled chestnuts, chopped

finely grated zest of 1 small lemon

25g fresh white breadcrumbs

1 tbsp chopped thyme leaves

freshly grated nutmeg

FOR THE PASTRY:

350g plain flour

90g chilled butter

90g chilled lard

1 medium free-range egg, beaten

1. Heat the oil and 15g of the butter in a large flameproof casserole. Brown the meat in batches, followed by the bacon and set aside on a plate. Add another 15g butter to the casserole with the onion, thyme and juniper and fry for 5 minutes until soft and lightly browned. Stir in the flour, then gradually add the stock, port, redcurrant jelly and bay leaves. Bring to the boil, stirring, then return the game and bacon, cover and leave to simmer gently for 1 hour.

2. Heat the remaining butter in a pan, add the carrots and celery and fry gently until lightly browned. Add to the casserole, and cook, covered for another 15 minutes, until the game and veg are tender.

3. Meanwhile, mix the ingredients for the stuffing balls together with some seasoning and shape into about 15 walnut-sized balls. Heat the sunflower oil in a frying pan and brown them lightly on all sides.

4. Using a slotted spoon, transfer the meat from the game mix into a deep, rimmed 2.5 litre pie dish. Reduce the cooking liquid to 500ml, pour back over the meat and leave to cool. Pop a pie funnel into the centre, then arrange the stuffing balls on top. Preheat the oven to 220°C/Gas 7.

5. For the pastry, sift the flour and 1 teaspoon salt into a food processor, add the butter and lard, and whiz until it resembles fine breadcrumbs. Add 3 tablespoons cold water and whiz until it comes together into a ball, then turn onto a lightly floured work surface and knead until smooth. Roll the pastry out until 2.5cm larger than the top of the pie dish, then cut a small cross in the centre. Cut a thin strip from around the edge of the pastry, brush with beaten egg and press onto the rim. Brush with more egg, then carefully lift the pastry onto the dish so that the funnel pokes through the cross. Seal the edges and trim away any excess pastry. Crimp the edges between your fingers, brush with more beaten egg and chill for 20-30 minutes, then brush again and bake for 30-35 minutes until the pastry is golden and the filling bubbling hot.

People are eating more and more venison here in Britain, and about time, too! It's sustainable, free-range, really good for you and has a gloriously rich, gamey flavour. What's not to love?

Or you could try...
Beef stew with macaroni gratin
Switch the venison for blade or chuck steak, adding the zest of ½ small orange and a cinnamon stick instead of the juniper. Omit the chestnuts and add 200g browned button onions and 50g black olives instead. To serve, mix 500g cooked macaroni with 250ml of the stew liquid and layer up in a gratin dish with 75g finely grated parmesan. Grill for 3-4 minutes until golden and bubbling.

Venison & red wine stew with herby dumplings

SERVES 6

1.5kg trimmed venison shoulder, cut into 4-5cm pieces

750ml full-flavoured red wine

6 garlic cloves, crushed

1 tsp juniper berries, crushed then roughly chopped

the leaves from 4 large thyme sprigs

6 fresh bay leaves

3 tbsp sunflower oil

60g butter

2 large onions, chopped

3 tbsp plain flour

600ml good beef, game or venison stock

1 tbsp tomato purée

2 tbsp crab apple, redcurrant or bramble jelly

200g cooked peeled chestnuts

1 tbsp apple balsamic vinegar

salt and freshly ground black pepper

FOR THE HERBY DUMPLINGS:

150g self-raising flour

½ tsp baking powder

½ tsp salt

75g shredded suet

the leaves from 2 thyme sprigs

1 tbsp chopped curly leaf parsley

1. Put the meat, wine, garlic, juniper, thyme and bay into a large bowl. Cover and marinate for 24-48 hours.

2. Drain the venison through a colander set over a bowl. Lift out the pieces of meat and pat dry well on kitchen paper. Return all the herbs to the marinade.

3. Season the meat well with salt and pepper. Heat 2 tablespoons of the oil in a large flameproof casserole over a medium-high heat and brown the venison in batches, spooning each batch onto a plate when done.

4. Pour away the excess oil from the casserole, add the butter and onion and cook over a medium heat until soft and richly golden. Stir in the flour, followed by the marinade, bring to the boil, stirring, and leave to simmer vigorously until reduced by half. Add the venison, stock, tomato purée, crab apple jelly, 1 teaspoon salt and plenty of black pepper and return to the boil. Simmer very gently, uncovered, for 1¾ hours, stirring occasionally, until the meat is almost tender and the liquid has reduced and thickened. Stir in the chestnuts and balsamic and season to taste.

5. For the dumplings, sift the flour, baking powder, salt and a little pepper into a bowl. Stir in the suet, thyme and parsley, followed by approximately 150ml water to make a soft, slightly sticky dough. Using a spoon, divide the mixture equally into 6 and drop, spaced apart, on top of the simmering stew. Cover and continue to simmer for a further 20 minutes, until the dumplings have puffed up and are cooked-through and the meat is tender. A fine skewer pushed into the centre of a dumpling should come out clean. Serve.

If you're using wild rabbit for this recipe, make sure to choose young ones as old rabbits can be tough as old boots. Farmed rabbit is delicious, too – look for 'Label Rouge' as this is the mark of a happy bunny.

Braised rabbit with cider, mustard & crème fraîche

SERVES 4-6

2 small young wild rabbits
(each weighing about 800-1kg)
OR 1 large farmed rabbit
(1.5-2kg), jointed

20g plain flour

2 tbsp sunflower oil

50g butter

2 tbsp cider vinegar

2 medium carrots, sliced

2 celery stalks, sliced

4 garlic cloves, sliced

the leaves from 1
large sprig thyme

the leaves from 2 x 13cm
sprigs rosemary, finely chopped

300ml dry fruity cider

1 tbsp Dijon mustard

50g crème fraîche

1 tbsp chopped parsley

salt and freshly
ground black pepper

1. Season the rabbit pieces and dust them lightly with the flour, knocking off and reserving the excess. Heat the oil and half the butter in a flameproof casserole or deep-sided sauté pan until foaming, add the rabbit pieces and brown them on all sides. Lift them into a shallow dish when they are done. Pour away the excess fat from the pan, add the cider vinegar and scrape the base with a wooden spoon to release all the caramelised bits and pieces. Pour over the rabbit and wipe the casserole clean.

2. Add the rest of the butter, carrot and celery to the casserole and fry for a few minutes until lightly browned. Add the garlic, thyme and rosemary and fry for 1 minute. Stir in the reserved flour, then the cider, and return the rabbit pieces to the casserole. Cover and simmer until tender; wild rabbit will take about 1-1¼ hours, farmed rabbit about 45 minutes.

3. Lift the rabbit into a warmed serving dish, cover and keep warm in a low oven. Increase the heat under the casserole or pan and simmer rapidly until the liquid is well-reduced and well-flavoured — about 5 minutes. Stir in the mustard and crème fraîche and simmer a little longer until the sauce has thickened again. Season to taste, stir in most of the parsley, and pour over the rabbit. Sprinkle over the remaining chopped parsley and serve with some buttery mash.

The recipe for the beetroot relish makes a tad more than you need for six burgers, but it'll keep in the fridge for two to three months and goes fabulously with all manner of cheeses and cold meats.

Venison burgers with apple balsamic & beetroot relish

SERVES 6

750g minced venison shoulder

250g minced belly pork

100g finely chopped shallots

the leaves from 3 thyme sprigs, roughly chopped

salt and coarsely ground black pepper

FOR THE APPLE BALSAMIC AND BEETROOT RELISH:

150ml cider vinegar

200ml apple balsamic vinegar

100g caster sugar

1 large red onion, chopped

500g peeled raw beetroot, cut into fine matchsticks

1 large Bramley apple

1 tsp lemon juice

salt

TO SERVE:

100g good mayonnaise

1 tbsp grated horseradish, fresh or from a jar

6 floury baps or bread rolls

lettuce leaves (red-tinged ones, such as ruby cos or oak leaf, look good)

½ cucumber, sliced

1. For the relish, bring the cider vinegar, apple balsamic and sugar to the boil, add the onion and simmer for 5–10 minutes until just tender. Add the beetroot and simmer for 15 minutes more until tender.

2. Meanwhile, peel and coarsely grate the apple. Stir in the apple, lemon juice and ½ teaspoon salt, bring to the boil and simmer, stirring frequently, for about 10 minutes until the mixture has thickened and most of the excess liquid has evaporated. Leave to cool, then spoon into warm sterilised jars with vinegar-proof lids for keeping.

3. For the burgers, put the minced venison and pork, shallots, thyme leaves, ¾ teaspoon salt and plenty of black pepper into a bowl and mix together well. Divide into 6 and shape into 2cm thick burgers.

4. Barbecue or griddle the burgers over a medium heat for 4–5 minutes on each side until nicely browned and cooked-through. Meanwhile, mix the mayo with the horseradish and a little seasoning. Split the rolls in half and spread the bottoms with mayo, then top with some lettuce leaves and cucumber. Pop the burgers on top of the lettuce, spoon over some beetroot relish and sandwich with the roll tops. Eat straight away.

Or you could try...

Pheasant, juniper & celery burgers. **Replace the** minced venison with minced pheasant meat, and use 75g minced streaky bacon and only 175g minced belly pork. Add 40g finely chopped central celery stalks to the mix and flavour with ½ tsp finely chopped juniper berries.

We still get a thrill from picking what we call 'hedgerow freebies'. If you live in the city, you might well find elder trees in your local park. They flower late May to mid-June, so keep your eyes peeled!

Elderflower, rhubarb and jelly creams

SERVES 8

FOR THE ELDERFLOWER AND RHUBARB JELLY:

200ml Elderflower cordial (see page 187)

1.5kg trimmed young pink rhubarb, cut into 2cm pieces

250g caster sugar

10g (about 5½ small sheets) leaf gelatine

FOR THE ELDERFLOWER CREAM:

300ml double cream

300ml whole milk

45g caster sugar

6 tbsp elderflower cordial

6g (about 3 small sheets) leaf gelatine

1. Put the elderflower cordial, rhubarb, sugar and 150ml water into a large pan, cover and cook gently over a medium-low heat for about 5 minutes until the fruit is soft but not falling apart. Tip the mixture into a muslin-lined sieve set over a bowl and leave to drain. You should end up with about 800ml juice. Set 600g of the cooked rhubarb aside in a mixing bowl.

2. For the jelly, soak the gelatine in a bowl of cold water for 5 minutes. Warm 150ml of the rhubarb juice in a small pan and take it off the heat. Lift the gelatine out of the water, squeeze out the excess water, add it to the warmed juice and leave it to dissolve. Stir this mix back into the rest of the rhubarb juice, then stir 6 tablespoons gently into the cooked rhubarb, reserving the rest. Spoon the rhubarb equally into 8 glass tumblers, cover and chill for 1 hour.

3. For the elderflower cream, put the cream, milk and sugar into a pan and warm very gently over a gentle heat to dissolve the sugar. Put the elderflower cordial in a small pan and warm this gently too. Meanwhile, soak the leaf gelatine in cold water for 5 minutes, remove, squeeze out the excess water and add it to the warmed cordial. Remove from the heat and leave to dissolve, then stir into the cream and milk.

4. Remove the tumblers from the fridge and pour over a layer of the cream. Chill for 2 hours or until set.

5. If the remaining rhubarb jelly has started to set, stand the pan in a little warm water until it dissolves again but don't let it get at all hot. Pour it over the top of the creams and return to the fridge one last time for at least 4 hours or until set.

Elderflower fritters with vanilla & honey yogurt

SERVES APPROX. 6

200g plain flour

1 medium free-range egg, beaten

300ml ice-cold sparkling water

1 tbsp grappa, or any
eau de vie (optional)

200g wholemilk natural yogurt

the seeds from 1 vanilla pod

1 tbsp clear honey

sunflower oil, for deep-frying

18-24 heads of freshly
picked elderflowers

icing sugar, for dusting

1. Sift the flour into a mixing bowl, make a well
   in the centre, add the egg and gradually whisk
   in the sparkling water to make a smooth batter.
   Whisk in the grappa if using. Cover and chill
   for 15-30 minutes.

2. Meanwhile, mix together the yogurt, vanilla seeds
   and honey in a small bowl. Heat a large, deep sauté
   pan with enough oil for deep-frying to 180°C.

3. Grab the elderflower heads one at a time by their
   stalks, dip them into the batter, then shake off
   the excess. Separate the clusters if necessary.
   Holding onto the stalk, lower each fritter into
   the hot oil and press down gently so that the
   clusters splay out. Leave to fry for 1½ minutes,
   then flip over and fry for another 1½ minutes.
   Drain briefly on kitchen paper and dust lightly
   with icing sugar. Serve with the vanilla and
   honey yogurt, but only dip sparingly or you
   will mask the flavour of the elderflowers.

Autumn berry & apple batter pudding

SERVES 6

4 dessert apples, such as
Cox's, peeled, quartered,
cored and diced

finely grated zest
and juice of 1 orange

185g caster sugar

700g mixed blackberries
and elderberries

2 tbsp cornflour, mixed
with 2 tbsp lemon juice

2 large free-range eggs

175g self-raising flour

pinch salt

100ml whole milk

100ml double cream

75g butter, melted and cooled

icing sugar, for dusting

1. Preheat the oven to 180°C/Gas 4. Put the apples,
   orange juice and 110g of the sugar in a pan and simmer
   for 5 minutes until the apples are almost tender.
   Add the mixed berries and simmer for about 3 minutes
   more until the berry juices start to run. Stir in the
   cornflour mix and simmer for a minute until thickened,
   then spoon the lot into a buttered, shallow, 2.5 litre
   ovenproof baking dish and leave to cool slightly.

2. Whisk the eggs and the remaining sugar together until
   thick and moussy. Whisk in the orange zest, then sift
   over half the flour and the salt and fold it in with
   half the milk and cream. Repeat once more, then fold
   in the melted butter.

3. Pour the mixture over the top of the berries and
   bake for 30 minutes until the pudding is firm to
   the touch and golden brown. Leave to cool slightly,
   then dust with icing sugar and serve warm with
   yogurt, clotted cream, custard or ice-cream.

Wild plums and damsons are not always easy to get hold of, but this fool works equally well with ordinary plums. Just make sure you stone them and cut them into wedges before cooking.

Wild plum or damson fool with sponge fingers

SERVES 4-6

300g wild plums or damsons

75g caster sugar

200ml double cream

FOR THE CUSTARD:

2 large free-range egg yolks

20g caster sugar

½ tsp vanilla bean paste or extract

100ml double cream

100ml whole milk

FOR THE SPONGE FINGERS (MAKES APPROX. 30):

3 large free-range eggs, separated

90g caster sugar

75g plain flour

6 tbsp icing sugar

1. For the custard, whisk the egg yolks, sugar and vanilla together in a bowl until thick and pale. Bring the cream and milk to the boil in a non-stick pan, then whisk into the yolk mixture. Return the lot to the pan and stir over a low heat until the mixture thickens and coats the back of a wooden spoon. Pour into a bowl and leave to cool, then chill for at least 4 hours.

2. Put the plums or damsons into a pan with the sugar and stir over a medium heat until the juices start to run, then increase the heat and cook for about 5 minutes, stirring occasionally, until cooked. Rub the mixture through a sieve into a bowl. Cool, then cover and chill along with the custard.

3. For the sponge fingers, preheat the oven to 180°C/ Gas 4. Beat the egg whites in a large clean bowl into soft peaks. Whisk in the caster sugar, one teaspoon at a time, to make a stiff and glossy meringue. Lightly beat the egg yolks and gently fold into the meringue, then sift over the flour and fold in. Spoon the mixture into a piping bag fitted with a 1cm plain nozzle and pipe 2cm wide strips in 8-10cm long lines across two large lined baking sheets, leaving 5cm between each one. Dust with half the icing sugar and leave to rest for 5 minutes, then dust with the remaining icing sugar and bake for 10 minutes. Leave to cool, then store in an airtight tin until needed.

4. To serve, whip the cream in a large mixing bowl until it just begins to form soft peaks. Gently fold in the custard and plum purée until only just mixed. Spoon into a serving bowl and serve with the sponge fingers for dipping.

Hedgerow cordial

This is a delicious way of using up foraged crab apples. Bramleys work just as well, mind.

MAKES APPROX. 1.75 LITRES

800g blackberries

600g elderberries

600g crab apples, washed and roughly chopped (in a food processor using the pulse button is quickest and easiest)

juice of 2 large lemons

granulated sugar (approx. 700g)

1. Pick over the fruit for leaves and bits, then pop them into a large pan with the lemon juice and 1 litre of cold water and bring slowly to the boil. Simmer for about 20 minutes until the fruit is very pulpy.

2. Leave to cool for 10 minutes, then tip into a large fine-meshed sieve set over a bowl and leave to drain, until the fruits have stopped dripping and have yielded about 1 litre of juice, about 2 hours.

3. Measure the syrup into a large, clean pan and add 700g of sugar to every litre of juice. Stir over a low heat until the sugar has completely dissolved. Pour immediately into warm sterilised bottles, leaving a 1cm gap at the top, seal and store in a cool, dark place or the fridge for up to 6 months.

Elderflower cordial

Just the thing for a hot day. We like to dilute with fizzy water, add a sprig of mint and a slice of lemon. Heaven!

MAKES APPROX. 2.5 LITRES

30-40 large elderflower heads

3 lemons

1.5kg granulated sugar

50g citric acid

1. If absolutely necessary, briefly rinse the flower heads to rid them of any bugs and shake them dry (or whiz them in a salad spinner). Put them into a large heatproof bowl. Grate the zest from the lemons, discard the ends and thinly slice the rest.

2. Put the sugar and 1.2 litres water into a large pan and bring slowly to the boil, stirring to dissolve the sugar. Stir in the citric acid, cool for 1-2 minutes, then pour the hot syrup over the flowers and stir in the lemon zest and slices. Leave to go cold, then cover and leave somewhere cool to steep for 24 hours.

3. Strain through a muslin-lined sieve and decant into sterilised bottles (leaving a 1cm gap at the top). Seal and store in a cool, dark place or the fridge for up to 6 months.

the fruit garden

Our favourite apples for eating — and juicing — would probably be a Ribston Pippin or an Ashmead's Kernel.

Somerset has an ideal climate for growing lots of different fruits, but we're probably most famous four our nice, juicy apples.

Fruit trees can take a few years to get going, but it's worth the wait: they'll keep on giving year after year.

The fresher the fruit is, the better it will taste, and the better for you it will be. Assuming it's perfectly ripe, of course!

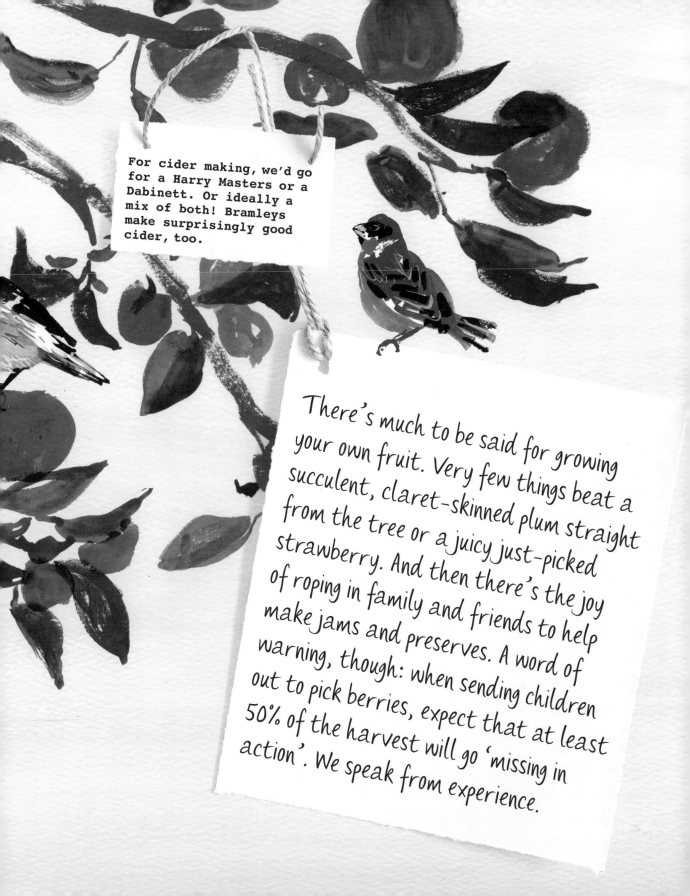

For cider making, we'd go for a Harry Masters or a Dabinett. Or ideally a mix of both! Bramleys make surprisingly good cider, too.

There's much to be said for growing your own fruit. Very few things beat a succulent, claret-skinned plum straight from the tree or a juicy just-picked strawberry. And then there's the joy of roping in family and friends to help make jams and preserves. A word of warning, though: when sending children out to pick berries, expect that at least 50% of the harvest will go 'missing in action'. We speak from experience.

Semifreddo is a delicious Italian-style ice-cream. The secret is to take it out of the freezer a few minutes before you need it – that way it will be lovely and soft. This recipe's made extra special thanks to some limoncello and crumbled meringues.

Eton mess semifreddo

SERVES 8

300g strawberries, hulled and halved

finely grated zest of 1 small lemon

6 tbsp limoncello or orange flavoured liqueur

3 large free-range eggs

50g caster sugar

300ml double cream

50g meringues (about 4 nests), crumbled into pieces

FOR THE STRAWBERRY SAUCE:

300g strawberries, hulled

2–3 tbsp icing sugar, depending on the sweetness of the berries

2 tsp lemon juice

2 tsp limoncello or orange-flavoured liqueur

1. For the semifreddo, put the strawberries, lemon zest and limoncello into a food processor and pulse into a coarse purée.

2. Separate the eggs into 2 large mixing bowls. Add the sugar to the yolks and whisk together until pale and really thick. Whisk the cream in an third bowl until it forms soft peaks. Whisk the egg whites into soft peaks.

3. Gently fold the cream into the egg yolks, followed by the strawberry purée, the egg whites and the crumbled meringues. Spoon the mixture into a 1.5 litre shallow serving dish. Cover with clingfilm and freeze until firm — at least 7–8 hours or overnight.

4. For the strawberry sauce, simply purée all the ingredients in a liquidiser until very smooth. Rub the mixture through a very fine sieve into a bowl, cover and chill until needed.

5. Leave the semifreddo to soften slightly at room temperature before serving. Scoop large spoonfuls onto dessert plates and drizzle over the sauce. Serve quickly as this melts faster than normal ice-cream.

Or you could try...

Gooseberry and meringue semifreddo. Gently cook 1kg gooseberries in a pan with 40g caster sugar and 6 elderflower heads until the juices run. Cover and cook for 5 minutes. Uncover, remove the elderflowers and stir in another 65–75g sugar. For the sauce, blend half the mixture in a liquidiser until really smooth, sieve into a bowl, stir in 2 tbsp elderflower cordial and chill. Simmer the remaining berries vigorously for 7–10 minutes until a thick purée. Stir in another 2 tbsp elderflower cordial and leave to cool. Use the purée and sauce in place of the strawberry versions.

Sharing can be nice enough, but there's something to be said for having a pud all to yourself. Especially when it's this incredibly classy trifle, with its beautiful layers of fruit, proper custard and brioche.

Summer pudding trifles

SERVES 4

75g blackcurrants

125g redcurrants, plus
4 sprigs to decorate

75g caster sugar

150g raspberries

100g small strawberries,
hulled and cut into small pieces

2 tbsp crème de cassis or
crème de framboise (optional)

half a 400-500g brioche loaf,
cut across into 8 slices
about 6mm thick

100g crème fraîche or lightly
whipped cream, to decorate

FOR THE CUSTARD:

½ vanilla pod, slit open
and the seeds scraped

75ml whole milk

75ml double cream

2 medium free-range egg yolks

15g caster sugar

7g cornflour

1. For the custard, put the vanilla pod and seeds into a small pan with the milk and cream and bring to the boil. Set aside for 20 minutes to infuse. Whisk the egg yolks and sugar together until pale and thick, then whisk in the cornflour. Return the milk to the boil, strain over the egg yolks and whisk in. Return the mix to the pan and cook over a low heat, stirring, until the custard is thick and coats the back of a spoon. Pour into a bowl and leave to go cold.

2. Put the blackcurrants and redcurrants into a pan with the sugar and 1 tablespoon water and cook gently for 2-3 minutes until the fruit soften and just burst. Take off the heat. Blend 1½ tablespoons of the currant juice with 50g of the raspberries until smooth, then rub them through a sieve into a bowl. Stir the raspberry purée back into the cooked currants with the rest of the raspberries, the diced strawberries and the liqueur, if using. Tip the mixture into a sieve set over a bowl and let about three-quarters of the juice drain away.

3. Cut a disc from each brioche slice using a pastry cutter, so that they fit snugly inside your chosen dessert glasses. Spoon some of the fruit mixture into the bottom of each glass. Dip half of the brioche discs, one at a time, into the berry syrup until well soaked, then lay on top of the fruit. Cover with the remaining fruit mixture and then the rest of the syrup-soaked brioche slices.

4. Pour the custard evenly over the trifles and chill for 2 hours, or until the custard has set. Decorate with the cream and redcurrant sprigs before serving.

We're lucky enough to have a few pear trees
on the farm, which is great as they're one of
our favourite fruits to cook with. Like apples,
they tend to go really well with spices.

Spiced pear bakewell

SERVES 8

FOR THE FILLING:

175g soft butter

175g caster sugar

2 large free-range eggs

40g self-raising flour

175g ground almonds

1 tsp vanilla extract

50g plain chocolate (about 70% cocoa solids), melted

2 ripe and juicy Conference pears

25g flaked almonds

FOR THE PASTRY:

225g plain flour

½ tsp ground cinnamon

pinch salt

65g icing sugar

125g chilled butter, cut into pieces

1 large free-range egg yolk, beaten together with 4 tsp ice-cold water

FOR THE GLAZE:

75g icing sugar

¼ tsp ground cinnamon

1. For the pastry, sift the flour, cinnamon, salt and icing sugar into a food processor. Add the butter and whiz until the mix looks like fine breadcrumbs. Pour over the egg yolk mixture and whiz briefly again until it starts to stick together. Tip it onto a lightly floured work surface, bring together into a ball and knead briefly until smooth. Roll out thinly and use to line a 23cm deep loose-bottomed flan tin, 4cm deep. Prick the base with a fork and chill for 20 minutes.

2. Put a baking sheet into the oven and preheat it to 200°C/Gas 6. Line the pastry case with foil, fill with a thin layer of baking beans and bake for 15 minutes until the edges are biscuit-coloured. Remove the beans and foil and return to the oven for 5-7 minutes until the pastry is crisp and golden brown. Set to one side. Lower the oven temperature to 170°C/Gas 3.

3. For the filling, beat the butter and sugar together in a bowl until light and fluffy. Beat in the eggs one at a time, adding a tablespoon of the flour with the second egg. Gently stir in the rest of the flour, the ground almonds and vanilla extract.

4. Spread the melted chocolate over the base of the pastry case. Peel, quarter and core the pears and cut each piece lengthways into 3 slices. Arrange them in a circle over the base of the case. Spoon the almond mixture over the top and spread evenly to the edges.

5. Put the tart onto the hot baking sheet and bake for 20 minutes. Carefully slide the oven shelf part-way out and sprinkle the flaked almonds over the top of the tart. Slide it back into the oven and bake for a further 30 minutes, covering loosely with foil towards the end of cooking if necessary, once it becomes nicely browned. Remove and leave to cool, then carefully remove from the tin.

6. For the glaze, sift the icing sugar and cinnamon into a small bowl and stir in 3 tsp warm water. Drizzle over the tart and leave to set before serving.

Why should the children have all the fun? Here are some truly decadent, grown-up jellies that look really handsome served in wine glasses. Just the thing for a party. A light and fruity British red would be perfect.

Blackcurrant & red wine jellies

SERVES 6

800g blackcurrants

300g caster sugar

500ml light and fruity red wine

14g leaf gelatine
(8 sheets)

custard (see page 195)
or ice-cold pouring
cream, to serve

1. Put the blackcurrants into a pan (there's no need to de-stalk them) with the sugar, red wine and 200ml water and slowly bring to a simmer, stirring to dissolve the sugar. Cook gently for 15 minutes. Then tip the mixture into a large, fine sieve set over another pan and leave to drain. This might take anything up to an hour, but don't squeeze out the juice or it will make your jellies cloudy. You should be left with 1 litre of intensely flavoured juice.

2. Soak the leaf gelatine in a large bowl of cold water for 5 minutes. Put the blackcurrant juice back over a low heat and gently warm through. Lift the gelatine out of the water, squeeze out the excess water and add to the pan. Stir until it has dissolved, then pour the mixture into 8 small dessert or wine glasses and chill for at least 6 hours or until set.

3. Pour some of the custard or cream on top of each jelly and serve.

Or you could try...

Damson, red wine & cinnamon jellies. Replace the blackcurrants with 1kg damsons and add a 10cm cinnamon stick to the fruit, red wine and sugar as they are cooking. Then continue as before. These are nice served with lightly whipped cream, flavoured with a little icing sugar and ground cinnamon.

The mighty crumble. Does it get more British than this? It certainly doesn't get much more delicious – especially when it's made with juicy plums and crunchy hazelnuts. Not to mention clotted cream!

Plum, oat & hazelnut crumbles with clotted cream

SERVES 6

900g plums

50g caster sugar, plus extra to sprinkle

½ tsp ground cinnamon

1 tbsp plain flour

clotted cream, to serve

FOR THE TOPPING:

75g self-raising flour

75g plain flour

95g chilled butter, cut into small pieces

50g caster sugar

25g demerara sugar

50g organic porridge oats (ideally not jumbo oats)

50g lightly toasted hazelnuts, roughly halved

pinch salt

1. For the topping, put the flours and butter into a food processor and whiz until the mixture looks like breadcrumbs. Add the caster sugar and pulse briefly until the mixture starts to stick together, then tip it into a shallow dish or baking tray. Add the demerara sugar, oats, hazelnuts and 1 tsp water and rake them through with a fork. Put in the freezer for 10 minutes or into the fridge until you're ready to bake.

2. Preheat the oven to 200°C/Gas 6. Halve the plums, remove the stones and cut the fruit into chunky wedges. Put the plums into a bowl with the sugar, cinnamon and flour and mix together well, then spoon into six 250ml deep baking dishes or mini pudding basins.

3. Spoon the crumble mixture generously over the fruit but don't press it down. Put them onto a baking tray and bake for 25 minutes until the fruit is hot and bubbling and the tops are richly golden. Remove and leave to sit for 5 minutes or so, then sprinkle with a little more caster sugar and serve with some clotted cream dolloped on top.

Or you could try...

Using any combination of seasonal fruits: 900g fresh fruit stoned, peeled, cored or de-stalked as necessary. Raspberry and apple is good, and so is peach and blackcurrant. Ring the changes with the nuts in the topping (almonds are lovely with apricot) and flavours with the fruit, such as elderflower with gooseberry. The possibilities are endless! Only use the flour in the filling with really watery fruits.

Grilling fruit is a brilliant way to bring out the flavour and it always looks impressive with its lightly charred edges. You don't have to make the shortbread fingers, but they do lend a nice crunch.

Lemon posset with sugar-grilled apricots & shortbread fingers

SERVES 4

300ml double cream

75g caster sugar

finely grated zest and juice of 1½ small lemons

FOR THE SUGAR-GRILLED APRICOTS:

4 ripe apricots

the seeds from ¼ vanilla pod

2 tbsp caster sugar

FOR THE LEMON SHORTBREAD FINGERS:

200g plain flour

45g ground almonds

45g semolina or ground rice

200g chilled butter, cut into pieces

finely grated zest of 1 large lemon

100g caster sugar, plus extra for sprinkling

1. For the posset, put the cream, sugar and lemon zest into a pan, bring to the boil and boil for exactly 3 minutes. Take off the heat, stir in the lemon juice then strain the mixture into a jug. Pour into teacups or ramekins and chill for at least 4 hours or until set.

2. For the shortbread, preheat the oven to 170°C/Gas 3 and grease a 20 x 25cm shallow loose-bottomed tin and line the base with non-stick paper. Put the flour, ground almonds and semolina into a food processor, add the cold butter and lemon zest and whiz until the mixture looks like fine breadcrumbs. Add the sugar and whiz briefly once more until the mixture just starts to stick together.

3. Tip the mixture into the tin and press out in an even layer. Bake for 25-30 minutes until a pale golden brown. Remove, mark the shortbread into 32 thin fingers, sprinkle generously with caster sugar and leave to cool. When cold, remove from the tin and carefully cut into fingers using a sharp, serrated knife.

4. Shortly before serving, preheat your grill as high as it will go. Halve the apricots, discard the stones and cut them into chunky wedges. Place them cut-side up on a baking tray dish. Mix the vanilla seeds into the sugar with your fingertips and then sprinkle a little over each apricot piece. Slide under the grill, as close to the heat source as you can, and grill for 3 minutes until they are hot and the sugar has started to caramelise. Put the apricots on top of the lemon possets and serve with the shortbread fingers.

Our farm cider...

starts with 100% apple juice. You can make cider from one single variety apple, but we like to use a mix. That way we get a nice, balanced drink that's not too tart and not too sweet. The main three cider apples we use are Harry Masters, Dabinett and Court de Wick. Not that dessert or eating apples don't make good cider too – they do! In fact, we like to blend our cider-apple juice with a spot of Ashmead's Kernel, Ribston Pippin or even bramley.

1. Pick apples at their ripest, when they start to fall from tree.

2. Mulch the apples. This means chopping them up quite roughly and we have a machine that does this.

3. Place the pummace (the chopped apples) in cloths and layer them between the wooden slats of an apple press, until there are about 5 layers.

4. Apply pressure to squeeze out the juice, collecting it in a bucket placed below the press.

5. Decant the juice into barrels and leave the tops open. During this time the natural yeasts from the apples will start the fermentation process.

6. When the juice starts to ferment, a frothy scum develops on the surface. We scrape this off each day and top up the liquid level with a little water until the juice stops 'working', meaning the fermentation has finished.

7. Tightly seal the barrels and let the cider mature, depending on the varieties and weather. It can take 3 to 6 months until the cider is ready to drink. Cheers!

We always look forward to the beginning of autumn. Yes the weather gets nippier and the days get shorter, but it's also when the apple season kicks in. And what could be cosier than a creamy rice pudding with some baked apples?

Nutmeg rice pudding with cider-baked apples

SERVES 6

750ml whole milk

200ml double cream

150g short-grain pudding rice

100g caster sugar

½ tsp freshly grated nutmeg

FOR THE CIDER-BAKED APPLES:

75g butter

50g each light and dark muscovado sugar

200g raisins or sultanas

2 tbsp honey

finely grated zest of 1 small orange

finely grated zest of 1 lemon

1 tsp ground allspice

1 tsp freshly grated nutmeg

½ tsp ground cinnamon

pinch ground cloves

6 small Bramley apples, each weighing about 200g

6 tbsp fruity vintage cider

1. For the baked apples, melt the butter, add both sugars and stir until there are no lumps. Stir in the dried fruit, honey, orange and lemon zest and spices and leave to go cold.

2. Preheat the oven to 190°C/Gas 5. Remove the cores from the apples with a corer then open up the cavity further with a small, sharp knife until the holes measure 3cm across. Take a small slice off the bottom if necessary so that they sit flat, then score a horizontal line through the skin around the middle of each one. Put them into a large baking dish and stuff the cavities with the fruit mixture. Pour the cider into the dish, cover loosely with foil and bake for 30 minutes. Uncover and cook for 10 minutes more, or until they are soft to the centre and lightly caramelised and the sauce is thick and bubbling.

3. Meanwhile, make the rice pudding. Put the milk, cream, rice, sugar and nutmeg into a pan, bring to the boil and leave to simmer for 30–35 minutes, stirring regularly, until the rice is tender and the mixture is creamy and thick. Remove from the heat and leave to rest for 5–10 minutes. Serve with the baked apples.

Or you could try...

Vanilla-roasted plums. Put 700g halved, stoned plums cut-side up in a shallow baking dish. Slit open 1 large vanilla pod, scrape out the seeds and add them to 50g caster sugar, then cut the pod into 4 pieces. Tuck the pod pieces in among the plums and scatter over the vanilla sugar. Drizzle over 3 tbsp water and bake as before for 30–45 minutes until the plums are tender and the juices are thick and syrupy.

If you love baked apples and you love custard, you'll adore this recipe – it brings the two together beautifully. It's one of the only recipes we've come across that has a set custard inside. Genius!

Warm apple, honey & vanilla custard pie

SERVES 8–10

FOR THE PASTRY:

350g plain flour

50g self-raising flour

50g cornflour

large pinch salt

275g chilled butter, cut into pieces

100g golden caster sugar

3 large egg yolks, beaten together with 1 tsp vanilla bean paste and 2 tbsp cold water

a little beaten egg, for sealing and brushing

2 tbsp granulated sugar, to decorate

FOR THE FILLING:

1.25kg dessert apples, such as Cox's, peeled, cored and thinly sliced

2 medium free-range eggs, plus 2 extra yolks

100g clear honey

1 tbsp self-raising flour

250ml double cream

1 tsp vanilla bean paste

extra cream or custard, to serve

1. Sift the flours, cornflour and salt into a food processor, add the butter and whiz until the mix resembles fine breadcrumbs. Stir in the caster sugar and egg yolk mix and whiz briefly until it starts to stick together. Turn out onto a floured surface and knead briefly until smooth. Cut off a 325g piece, wrap it in clingfilm and set to one side.

2. Roll the remaining dough out thinly on a lightly floured surface into a 30cm disc and use to line a greased 23cm loose-bottomed flan tin, 4cm deep, leaving the edges overhanging. Chill for 20 minutes. Knead the pastry trimmings with the second piece of pastry, wrap in clingfilm and chill alongside the pastry case. Meanwhile, preheat the oven to 170°C/Gas 3.

3. Line the pastry case with foil, cover with a thin layer of baking beans and bake for 20 minutes. Remove the foil and baking beans and return to the oven for another 10 minutes until lightly golden. Leave to cool.

4. Put the sliced apples in a large mixing bowl. Whisk the eggs, yolks, honey and flour in a jug until smooth, then whisk in the cream and vanilla paste. Pour over the apples and stir together well. Spoon the lot into the pastry case, trying to make sure it's as level as possible and slightly domed in the centre.

5. Re-knead and roll out the remaining pastry into a 25cm disc. Brush the edges with beaten egg, lift over the case and press the edges together to seal. Make a small hole in the lid's centre, brush with egg and sprinkle with granulated sugar. Bake for about 1½ hours, covering with foil once nicely browned, until the apples are tender when pierced with a skewer and the custard has set. Leave to cool for 30 minutes before serving.

This makes more jam than you need for one cake, but it'll keep in the fridge for a few weeks and is great stirred into yogurt, on scones or, of course, on hot buttered toast.

Or you could try... Strawberry, rhubarb and elderflower cake. Replace the raspberry jam with Strawberry and rhubarb jam (see page 72). Whip the cream with 2 tbsp elderflower cordial (see page 187). Mix 100g of icing sugar with 4 tsp elderflower cordial and 1-1½ tsp warm water, spread over the top of the cake and leave to set before cutting.

Sponge cake with baked raspberry jam & lemon cream

SERVES 8

30g butter, melted and cooled, plus extra for greasing

190g plain flour, plus extra for dusting

4 large free-range eggs

300g caster sugar

1 tsp baking powder

pinch salt

icing sugar, for dusting

FOR THE BAKED RASPBERRY JAM:

500g firm and really ripe raspberries

500g caster sugar

2 tsp lemon juice

FOR THE LEMON CREAM:

200ml very fresh whipping or double cream

2 tbsp icing sugar

finely grated zest of 1 small lemon

2 tsp lemon juice

1. For the jam, preheat the oven to 180°C/Gas 4. Spread the raspberries in a thin layer over the base of one medium-sized ovenproof dish and the sugar in another. Pop them in the oven and bake for 30 minutes, until they are really hot but the fruit is still holding its shape. Quickly stir the sugar into the raspberries with the lemon juice, spoon into a bowl and leave to cool, then cover and chill until needed.

2. Lightly grease two 24cm sandwich tins with melted butter, line the bases with non-stick baking paper, grease again and then dust with flour, knocking out the excess. Increase the oven temperature to 190°C/Gas 5.

3. Separate the eggs into 2 large mixing bowls. Beat the yolks and sugar together for 2 minutes, then add 100ml warm water and whisk for another 10 minutes until thick and moussy. Sift the flour, baking powder and salt together and gently fold in with a large spoon in 3 batches, then fold in the melted butter. Whisk the egg whites into soft peaks and gently fold in.

4. Pour the mixture equally into the prepared cake tins and bake for 18-20 minutes until firm to the touch, golden and just beginning to shrink away from the sides of the tins. Turn the cakes out immediately onto a wire rack, flip them over and leave to cool.

5. When you are ready to assemble the cake, place one sponge top-side down onto a cake plate and spread with 6-8 tablespoons of the jam. Whip the cream with the icing sugar, lemon zest and juice into soft peaks and spread onto the base of the other. Flip over onto the top of the raspberry sponge and dust with icing sugar.

We either eat this cake hot, straight from the oven, as a pudding with custard, or leave it to go cold to serve with cups of tea. Bring back elevenses, we say!

Or you could try... Plum, lemon and cinnamon cake. Replace the orange zest with lemon zest and the rhubarb with the same weight of stoned and thickly sliced ripe but firm plums. Switch the ginger for cinnamon in the topping.

Rhubarb, orange & hazelnut cake

SERVES 8-10

250g prepared rhubarb, cut into 4cm lengths

350g golden caster sugar

finely grated zest and juice of 1 large orange

200g skinned hazelnuts

150g self-raising flour

1 tsp baking powder

300g unsalted butter, softened

4 medium free-range eggs

FOR THE TOPPING:

50g butter

50g light muscovado sugar

½ tsp ground ginger

100g skinned hazelnuts, roughly chopped

1. Mix the rhubarb with 50g of the caster sugar and half the orange zest. Cover and set aside for 20 minutes. Grease a 20 x 25cm shallow cake tin and line with baking paper. Preheat the oven to 190°C/Gas 5.

2. Put the hazelnuts into a food processor and whiz until finely chopped. Add the flour and baking powder and whiz together until very finely ground.

3. Cream the butter, remaining sugar and orange zest together until pale and fluffy. Beat in the eggs, one at a time, then fold in the hazelnut and flour mixture and 4 tablespoons of the orange juice. Spoon the mixture into the prepared cake tin and level the surface, then spoon the rhubarb pieces evenly over the top. Bake for 25 minutes.

4. Meanwhile, for the topping, melt the butter in a small pan, then stir in the sugar, ground ginger and hazelnuts and mix together well.

5. Remove the part-cooked cake from the oven and scatter the topping evenly over the top. Return the cake to the oven, reduce the oven temperature to 180°C/Gas 4 and bake for a further 20 minutes, until a skewer inserted into the centre of the cake comes away clean. Leave to cool in the tin, then remove and serve cut into squares.

The quince, once a favourite of the Victorian garden, has fallen slightly out of favour of late. But we're very fond of it. If you can't track them down, don't fret – firm pears or dessert apples such as russets or Cox's will do brilliantly.

Quince & ginger upside down pudding

SERVES 8

900g–1kg quinces
(about 4–5 large fruit)

175g caster sugar

170g unsalted butter

100g plain flour

2 tsp ground ginger

1 tsp ground cinnamon

¼ tsp ground cloves

¼ tsp freshly grated nutmeg

¼ tsp salt

50g light muscovado sugar

3 large free-range eggs

125g golden syrup

1 tbsp finely grated
fresh root ginger

1 tsp bicarbonate of soda

1. Peel, quarter and core the quinces, then cut them into 1cm thick wedges and drop them into a bowl of lemon water. Preheat the oven to 180°C/Gas 4.

2. Put the sugar and 4 tablespoons water into a large frying pan and dissolve over a low heat. Bring to the boil and cook for 3–4 minutes until amber-caramel in colour. Remove from the heat, add 50g of the butter and swirl the pan until it has melted and mixed in.

3. Drain and dry the quince slices, then add to the pan. Cook them for 7–8 minutes, carefully turning now and then, until just tender when pierced with a knife. Using a slotted spoon, spoon the fruit over the base of a lightly buttered, shallow, 23cm cake tin. Return the syrup to the heat and boil until reduced and thickened. Pour the mixture over the quinces and leave to cool.

4. Sift the flour, spices and salt into a bowl. Beat the remaining butter in a bowl until pale and fluffy. Add the muscovado sugar and beat for 3 minutes, then gradually beat in the eggs. The mixture will curdle, but don't worry. Beat in the golden syrup and grated ginger, then gently mix in half of the flour mixture. Mix the bicarb with 2 tablespoons boiling water, beat into the mixture then add the remaining flour. Pour over the quinces and bake for 15 minutes until the pudding is well-coloured. Cover loosely with foil, lower the oven to 170°C/Gas 3 and cook for a further 25–30 minutes until a skewer pushed into the centre of the cake comes out clean.

5. Leave the cake to cool in the tin for 10 minutes, then turn it out onto a serving plate and serve.

The gooseberry – another woefully underused British fruit. Raw, they do seem a bit unpromising: hard, hairy and face-scrunchingly sour. But when slowly cooked with sugar they really come into their own.

Gooseberry & lemon meringue pies

MAKES 8 INDIVIDUAL TARTS

FOR THE PASTRY:

225g plain flour

¼ tsp salt

65g icing sugar

125g chilled unsalted butter, cut into small pieces

1 large free-range egg yolk, beaten together with 4 tsp ice-cold water

FOR THE FILLING:

900g gooseberries, topped and tailed

finely grated zest and juice of 1 lemon

150g caster sugar

2 tbsp cornflour, mixed together with 2 tbsp cold water

3 large free-range egg yolks

50g unsalted butter

FOR THE MERINGUE:

3 large free-range egg whites

175g caster sugar

1. For the pastry, sift the flour, salt and icing sugar into a food processor. Add the butter and whiz until the mixture resembles fine breadcrumbs. Add the egg yolk mix to the bowl and pulse briefly until it begins to stick together. Turn out onto a lightly floured surface and knead until smooth, then cut into 8 pieces and chill for 15 minutes. Thinly roll out the pastry and use to line 8 buttered 10cm tart cases, 4cm deep. Line the cases with foil and chill for another 15 minutes.

2. Preheat the oven to 200°C/Gas 6. Fill the chilled tart cases with baking beans and bake for 15 minutes. Remove the foil and beans and bake for another 3–5 minutes or until the bases are golden brown. Set aside.

3. Meanwhile, make the filling. Put the gooseberries in a pan with 2 tablespoons lemon juice and the sugar. Cover and simmer gently for about 15 minutes, stirring occasionally, until just tender. Tip into a sieve set over a pan to drain, then simmer the juice vigorously until reduced to about 200ml. Stir the cornflour mix in with the drained gooseberries and lemon zest and simmer for 2 minutes, stirring, until thick. Remove from the heat, cool slightly then stir in the egg yolks and butter. Spoon into the tart cases and leave to cool.

4. Reduce the oven temperature to 170°C/Gas 3. Whisk the egg whites in a large clean bowl into medium-stiff peaks, then whisk in the sugar a tablespoon at a time to make a stiff, glossy meringue. Spread it evenly over the tarts, then swirl with the tip of a knife. Bake for 15 minutes until lightly browned. Serve warm or cold.

This is a very clever recipe because you use the egg whites for the pavlova meringue and the yolks for the curd: very good housekeeping indeed. If you can't come by cobnuts, hazelnuts will be dandy.

Cobnut pavlovas with passion fruit curd

SERVES 4

150g cobnuts in their shells or 40g shelled and skinned hazelnuts

3 large, very fresh free-range egg whites

pinch salt

175g caster sugar

1 tsp cornflour

½ tsp white wine vinegar

150ml double cream, lightly whipped, to serve

the pulp from 4 ripe and wrinkly passion fruit, to serve

FOR THE PASSION FRUIT CURD:

the pulp from 12 large, ripe and wrinkly passion fruit

3 large free-range eggs, plus 3 extra yolks

3 large free-range egg yolks

175g caster sugar

120g unsalted butter

1. For the curd, scoop the passion fruit pulp into a pan and bring to a gentle simmer. Take off the heat and stir for about 5 minutes, then tip into a sieve set over a bowl and rub out the juice with a wooden spoon. You should be left with about 200ml juice.

2. Put the eggs, egg yolks, passion fruit juice, sugar and butter into a heatproof bowl. Place over a pan of just simmering water and stir continuously for about 15 minutes until the curd has thickened and leaves behind a visible trail when drizzled back over the surface. Pour into two sterilised 350g jars, cover with waxed jam discs, leave to cool, then seal. It will keep in the fridge for 3–4 weeks.

3. For the pavlovas, preheat the oven to 200°C/Gas 6. Spread the cobnuts onto a baking tray and roast for 25–30 minutes or until crunchy. (Hazelnuts will only need 6–7 minutes.) Leave to cool, then chop roughly. Lower the oven temperature to 140°C/Gas 1.

4. Whisk the egg whites in a large bowl with a pinch of salt into stiff peaks. Gradually whisk in the sugar, a spoonful at a time, to make a stiff and shiny meringue, then whisk in the cornflour and vinegar. Stir in the chopped nuts.

5. Drop 4 large spoonfuls of the mixture onto 2 baking trays lined with baking paper and shape into 10cm rounds with the back of the spoon, making a slight dip in the centre. Bake for 40–45 minutes until pale. Turn off the oven and leave them to cool inside.

6. To serve, spoon some of the whipped cream into the hollow of each pavlova, drizzle over some of the passion fruit curd, then spoon over the pulp. Serve immediately, before the meringue starts to go soft.

Recipe List

Breakfasty bits

Apple & honey bircher muesli with fruit & nuts.. 51

Buttermilk pancakes with honey & vanilla butter. 53

Caramelised oatmeal, Somerset cider brandy
& honey creams with blueberries 34

Cheddar farls with fried eggs & crispy bacon ... 54

Crunchy apple & raspberry granola 51

Milk & honey jellies with honeycomb & cream 34

Soups

Celery & stilton soup with hot potato scones ... 23

Cream of asparagus soup with soft-poached eggs . 78

Field mushroom soup 163

Slow-roasted tomato soup with chilli
& cheese cornmeal muffins 81

Salads

Apple, celery, fennel & spelt salad with
cranberries & pomegranate molasses dressing..... 85

Autumn salad with pears, pomegranate seeds,
blue cheese & caramelised walnuts 86

Farmer's salad of fried new potatoes,
duck eggs & black pudding 108

Orange-roasted beetroot salad with
goats' cheese & dill 89

Summer green tabbouleh 90

Warm English chicken salad with
creamy tarragon salad cream 123

Starters, snacks & light dishes

Broad bean paté on toast with torn mozzarella,
basil, & lemon oil 82

Carrot & coriander fritters
with green yogurt sauce 94

Coarse game & green peppercorn terrine 168

Chicken liver & cider brandy parfait 117

Field mushrooms in garlic & parsley butter
on granary toast with crispy bacon 162

Herby Scotch eggs with sage & lemon 112

Hot salt beef sandwich on rye with
mustard & gherkin tartare & leaves 134

Trout & fennel gravlax with mustard
& horseradish sauce 164

Twice-baked goats' cheese soufflés
with radish & watercress salad 27

Main dishes - Veggie

Beetroot, new potato & crème fraîche pies 95

Blue cheese & leek tart
in cheesy oatmeal pastry 28

Cauliflower, caramelised
red onion & Caerphilly cake 114

Cauliflower cheese with
roasted cherry tomatoes 99

Courgette, tomato & roasted red pepper gratin ... 97

Roasted squash, red onion,
green leaf & cheese tart 92

Spinach, wild garlic & filo pie 160

Swish chard, ricotta & lemon cannelloni 24

Fishy

Deep trout fishcakes with lemon butter
& chive sauce 31

Whole baked trout with crunchy
bacon & hyssop stuffing 167

Birdy

Chicken & mushroom lasagne 124

Chicken braised in local red wine
with mushrooms & smoky bacon 120

Crunchy parmesan & garlic 'picnic' chicken 114

Honey-roasted goose with spiced apple
sauce & port gravy 128

Pan-fried duck breasts with redcurrant
& orange sauce 127

Pot-roasted chicken with apples & cider 118

Roasted pheasant with pearl barley
& mushroom risotto 170

Slow-roasted chicken with thyme, lemon & garlic 121

Souffléd egg & bacon tart 111

Meaty

A hearty kale, white bean & sausage stew 102

Beef & barley cottage pie 140

Braised rabbit with cider,
mustard & crème fraiche 177

Braised steak in ale with
a herby cobbler topping 137

Grilled lamb chops with devilled kidneys 153

Marmalade-glazed gammon
with chunky potato gratin 144

Mixed game pie with sausagemeat-stuffing balls . 175
Our favourite Sumatran lamb curry 154

Roast rib of beef with a mustard flour crust ... 138
Slow-roasted pork with butter-roasted apples,
lemony carrots & cider gravy 143
Smoky bacon meatballs with pappardelle pasta .. 148
Sweet 'n' smoky pork chops with cabbage & mash 146
Venison & red wine stew with herby dumplings .. 176
Venison burgers with apple balsamic
& beetroot relish 179
Warm lamb salad with a pea, mint &
feta cheese dressing 101

Puds

Autumn berry & apple batter pudding 183
Blackcurrant & red wine jellies 198
Cobnut pavlovas with passion fruit curd 216
Deep-filled nutmeg & custard tart 41
Elderflower fritters with
vanilla & honey yogurt 183
Elderflower, rhubarb & jelly creams 180
Eton mess semifreddo 192
Floating islands with red summer berries 43
Gooseberry & lemon meringue pies 215
Lemon curd & raisin bread & butter pudding 38
Lemon posset with sugar-grilled apricots
& shortbread fingers 203
Nutmeg rice pudding with cider-baked apples ... 206
Orange yogurt cheese cheesecake 32
Poppy seed & lemon ice cream
cake with stewed blackcurrants 37
Plum, oat & hazelnut
crumbles with clotted cream 200
Quince & ginger upside down pudding 214
Summer pudding trifles 195
Warm apple, honey & vanilla custard pie 209
Wild plum or damson fool with sponge fingers ... 184

Tea time treats

Blackberry & brown sugar fingers 64
Farmhouse fruit cake 60
Ginger cake with fudgy frosting 67
Honeycomb & chocolate biscuit cake 63

Raspberry, lemon & yogurt tea loaf 44
Redcurrant & white chocolate blondies 61
Rhubarb, orange & hazelnut cake 213
Somerset scrumpy & apple cake 59
Spiced pear bakewell 196
Sponge cake with baked
raspberry jam & lemon cream 210
White chocolate, yogurt
& sour cherry scones 56

Breads

Somerset cider, honey, walnut & raisin bread ... 70
Stoneground soda bread 68

Preserves & cordials

Elderflower cordial 187
Hedgerow cordial 187
Quince & orange marmalade 71
Sticky onion & raisin chutney 117
Strawberry & rhubarb jam 72

Notes

Eggs are free-range and medium unless otherwise stated; herbs are fresh; salt is sea salt, and pepper is freshly ground black pepper unless otherwise suggested. Use unwaxed lemons for grating and zesting. Spoon measures are level.

Anyone who is pregnant or in a vulnerable health group should avoid recipes that use raw egg whites or lightly cooked eggs.

Cooking times used are based on a conventional oven. If you are using a fan-assisted oven, set the temperature to 10° to 15° lower than called for in the recipe.

We believe that seasonal, locally produced food simply tastes better, so try and buy local wherever possible.

Index

A

apples

Apple and honey bircher muesli 51

Apple balsamic and beetroot relish 179

Apple, celery, fennel and spelt salad 85

Autumn berry and apple batter pudding 183

Butter-roasted apples 143

Cider-baked apples 206

Crunchy apple and raspberry granola 51

Somerset scrumpy and apple cake 59

Spiced apple sauce 128

Warm apple, honey and vanilla custard pie 209

Apricots, Sugar-grilled 203

Asparagus soup with soft-poached eggs 78

Aubergine gratin 97

Autumn berry and apple batter pudding 183

Autumn salad with pears, pomegranate seeds,
blue cheese and caramelised walnuts 86

B

bacon

Smoky bacon meatballs with pappardelle pasta .. 148

Souffléd egg and bacon tart 111

Banana milk shake 20

beef

Beef and barley cottage pie 140

Braised steak in ale with herby cobbler topping 137

Cheesy Italian polpetti meatballs 148

Hot salt beef sandwich on rye 134

Roast rib of beef with a mustard flour crust .. 138

Smoky bacon meatballs with pappardelle pasta .. 148

beetroot

Apple balsamic and beetroot relish 179

Beetroot, new potato and crème fraîche pies 95

Orange-roasted beetroot salad with goats'
    cheese and dill 89

Roasted beetroot, pomegranate and rocket salad . 89

blackberries

Autumn berry and apple batter pudding 183

Blackberry and brown sugar fingers 64

Hedgerow cordial 187

Blackcurrant and red wine jellies 198

Blue cheese and leek tart 28

Blue cheese butter 17

bread

Cheesy oat bread 68

Quick rye bread 70

Rosemary and olive bread 68

Somerset cider, honey, walnut and raisin bread.. 70

Stoneground soda bread 68

Sun-dried tomato and thyme bread 68

Broad bean pâté on toast 82

Butter 17

Flavoured butters 17

Buttermilk pancakes with honey and vanilla butter.. 53

butternut squash *see* **squash**

C

cabbage

Buttered caraway and garlic cabbage 146

cakes

Cauliflower, caramelised red onion
    and Caerphilly cake 114

Farmhouse fruit cake 60

Ginger cake with fudgy frosting 67

Honeycomb and chocolate biscuit cake 63

Pear, pecan and date cake 59

Plum, lemon and cinnamon cake 213

Raspberry, lemon and yogurt tea loaf 44

Rhubarb, orange and hazelnut cake 213

Somerset scrumpy and apple cake 59

Sponge cake with baked raspberry jam
    and lemon cream 210

Strawberry, rhubarb and elderflower cake 210

Caramelised oatmeal, Somerset cider brandy
and honey creams with blueberries 34

carrots

Carrot and coriander fritters
    with green yogurt sauce 94

Lemony carrots 143

Cauliflower, caramelised red onion
and Caerphilly cake 114

Cauliflower cheese with roasted cherry
tomatoes and crispy bacon 98

Celeriac mash 146

Celery and Stilton soup 23

chard *see* **Swiss chard**

Cheddar farls with fried eggs and crispy bacon 54

cheese (*see also* ricotta)

Blue cheese and leek tart in cheesy
    oatmeal pastry 28

Blue cheese butter 17

Cauliflower cheese with roasted cherry
    tomatoes and crispy bacon 98

Celery and Stilton soup 23

Cheddar farls with fried eggs and crispy bacon.. 54

Cheesy oat bread 68

Chilli and cheese cornmeal muffins 81

Cream cheese 18

Roasted squash, red onion, green leaf
    and cheese tart 92

Twice-baked goats' cheese soufflés 27

chicken

Chicken and mushroom lasagne 124

Chicken braised in local red wine
    with mushrooms and smoky bacon 120

Chicken stock 120

Crunchy parmesan and garlic 'picnic' chicken .. 114

Pot-roasted chicken with apples and cider 118

Slow-roasted chicken with thyme,
    lemon and garlic 121

Warm English chicken salad with
    tarragon salad cream 123

Chicken liver and cider brandy parfait 117
Chilli and cheese cornmeal muffins 81
chocolate
    Choc chip cookies 49
    Chocolate milk shake 20
    Dark chocolate and raspberry brownies 61
    Honeycomb and chocolate biscuit cake 63
    Redcurrant and white chocolate blondies 61
    White chocolate, yogurt and sour cherry scones . 56
Chutney, Sticky onion and raisin 117
Cider 204
Clotted cream 20
Clotted cream ice-cream 20
Cobnut pavlovas with passion fruit curd 216
Courgette, tomato and roasted red pepper gratin ... 97
Cream cheese 18
Cream cheese hearts with vanilla sugar 18
Crème fraîche 19
Curry, Lamb 154

D
Damson fool with sponge fingers 184
Duck breasts with redcurrant and orange sauce 127
Dumplings, Herby 176

E
eggs
    Cream of asparagus soup with soft-poached eggs . 78
    Farmer's salad of fried new potatoes,
        duck eggs and black pudding 108
    Herby Scotch eggs with sage and lemon 112
    Souffléd egg and bacon tart 111
elderberries
    Autumn berry and apple batter pudding 183
    Hedgerow cordial 187
Elderflower cordial 187
Elderflower fritters with vanilla and honey yogurt. 183
Elderflower, rhubarb and jelly creams 180
Eton Mess semifreddo 192

F
Farmhouse fruit cake 60
Fennel seed, chilli and garlic butter 17
Feta and roasted red pepper dip 15

G
game (see also pheasant; rabbit; venison)
    Coarse game and green peppercorn terrine 168
    Gamey devils on horseback 168
    Mixed game pie with sausage meat-stuffing balls. 175
gammon
    Marmalade glazed gammon with
        chunky potato gratin 144
Ginger cake with fudgy frosting 67
goose
    Honey-roasted goose with spiced apple sauce ... 128

Gooseberry and lemon meringue pies 215
Gooseberry and meringue semifreddo 192
Granola, Crunchy apple and raspberry 51

H
Hedgerow cordial 187
Herby dumplings 176
Herby Scotch eggs with sage and lemon 112
Honeycomb and chocolate biscuit cake 63

I
ice-cream
    Clotted cream ice-cream 20
    Eton Mess semifreddo 192
    Gooseberry and meringue semifreddo 192
    Lemon and cornflake ice-cream cake 37
    Poppy seed and lemon ice-cream cake 37

J
Jam, Strawberry and rhubarb 72

K
Kale, white bean and sausage stew 102
Kidneys, Devilled 153

L
lamb
    Griddled lamb chops with devilled kidneys 153
    Roast leg of lamb with rosemary
        and garlic 'pesto' 149
    Sumatran lamb curry 154
    Warm lamb salad with a pea,
        mint and feta cheese dressing 101
leeks
    Blue cheese and leek tart in
        cheesy oatmeal pastry 28
Lemon and cornflake ice-cream cake 37
Lemon curd and raisin bread and butter pudding 38
Lemon posset with sugar-grilled apricots 203
Lemon shortbread fingers 203

M
Marmalade, Quince and orange 71
Marmalade glazed gammon with chunky potato gratin. 144
meringue
    Cobnut pavlovas with passion fruit curd 216
    Eton Mess semifreddo 192
    Gooseberry and lemon meringue pies 215
    Gooseberry and meringue semifreddo 192
Milk and honey jellies with honeycomb and cream .. 34
Milk shakes 20
Muesli, Apple and honey bircher 51
Muffins, Chilli and cheese cornmeal 81
mushrooms
    Chicken and mushroom lasagne 124
    Field mushroom soup 163

Field mushrooms in garlic and parsley butter .. 162
Pearl barley and mushroom risotto 170

N
Nutmeg and custard tart 41
Nutmeg rice pudding with cider-baked apples 206

O
onions
    Cauliflower, caramelised red onion
       and Caerphilly cake 114
    Sticky onion and raisin chutney 117
oranges
    Orange-roasted beetroot salad with
       goats' cheese and dill 89
    Orange yogurt cheese cheesecake 32
    Quince and orange marmalade 71

P
Pancakes, buttermilk with honey
    and vanilla butter, ... 53
pasta
    Chicken and mushroom lasagne 124
    Smoky bacon meatballs with pappardelle pasta .. 148
    Swiss chard, ricotta and lemon cannelloni 24
    Tagliatelle with crème fraîche,
       butter and cheese 19
peaches *see* **Plum crumbles**
Peanut butter milk shake 20
pears
    Autumn salad with pears, pomegranate seeds,
       blue cheese and caramelised walnuts 86
    Pear, pecan and date cake 59
    Spiced pear Bakewell 196
peppers
    Feta and roasted red pepper dip 15
pheasant (*see also* **game**)
    Pheasant, juniper and celery burgers 179
    Roasted pheasant with pearl barley
       and mushroom risotto 170
plums
    Plum, lemon and cinnamon cake 213
    Plum, oat and hazelnut crumbles 200
    Vanilla-roasted plums 206
    Wild plum fool with sponge fingers 184
Poppy seed and lemon ice-cream cake
    with stewed blackcurrants 37
pork
    Slow-roasted pork with butter roasted apples .. 143
    Sweet 'n' smoky pork chops with
       cabbage and mash 146
potatoes
    Celeriac mash 146
    Chunky potato gratin 144
    Farmer's salad of fried new potatoes,
       duck eggs and black pudding 108
    Hot potato scones 23

Q
Quince and ginger upside down pudding 214
Quince and orange marmalade 71

R
rabbit (*see also* **game**)
    Braised rabbit with cider,
       mustard and crème fraîche 177
raspberries
    Crunchy apple and raspberry granola 51
    Dark chocolate and raspberry brownies 61
    Floating islands with red summer berries 43
    Raspberry, lemon and yogurt tea loaf 44
    Sponge cake with baked raspberry
       jam and lemon cream 210
    Summer pudding trifles 195
redcurrants
    Floating islands with red summer berries 43
    Redcurrant and orange sauce 127
    Redcurrant and white chocolate blondies 61
    Summer pudding trifles 195
rhubarb
    Elderflower, rhubarb and jelly creams 180
    Rhubarb, orange and hazelnut cake 213
    Strawberry and rhubarb jam 72
    Strawberry, rhubarb and elderflower cake 210
Rice pudding, Nutmeg 206
Ricotta 16
    Baked ricotta with thyme 16
    Swiss chard, ricotta and lemon cannelloni 24
risotto
    Pearl barley and mushroom risotto 170
Rosemary and garlic 'pesto' 149
Rosemary and olive bread 68

S
salads
    Apple, celery, fennel and spelt salad 85
    Autumn salad with pears, pomegranate seeds,
       blue cheese and caramelised walnuts 86
    Farmer's salad of fried new potatoes,
       duck eggs and black pudding 108
    Orange-roasted beetroot salad ....
       with goats' cheese and dill 89
    Radish and watercress salad 27
    Roasted beetroot, pomegranate and rocket salad.. 89
    Summer green tabbouleh 90
    Warm English chicken salad with
       tarragon salad cream 123
    Warm lamb salad with a pea,
       mint and feta cheese dressing 101
sauces
    Green yogurt 94
    Lemon butter and chive 31
    Mustard and gherkin tartare 134
    Mustard and horseradish 164
    Redcurrant and orange 127
    Spiced apple 128
    Tomato 148
sausages
    Kale, white bean and sausage stew 102
scones
    Hot potato scones 23
    White chocolate, yogurt and sour cherry scones.. 56

Soda bread, Stoneground 68
Somerset cider, honey, walnut and raisin bread 70
Somerset scrumpy and apple cake 59
Soufflés, Twice-baked goats' cheese 27
soups
    Celery and Stilton soup 23
    Cream of asparagus soup with soft-poached eggs.. 78
    Field mushroom soup 163
    Slow-roasted tomato soup 81
Spinach, wild garlic and filo pie 160
Sponge fingers 184
Squash, red onion, green leaf and cheese tart 92
strawberries
    Eton Mess semifreddo 192
    Floating islands with red summer berries 43
    Strawberry and rhubarb jam 72
    Strawberry milk shake 20
    Summer pudding trifles 195
Summer green tabbouleh 90
Summer pudding trifles 195
Swiss chard, ricotta and lemon cannelloni 24

T
Tagliatelle with crème fraîche, butter and cheese.. 19
Tarragon and garlic butter 17
tomatoes
    Courgette, tomato and roasted red pepper gratin. 97
    Slow-roasted tomato soup 81
    Sun-dried tomato and thyme bread 68
    Sun-dried tomato, rosemary and olive butter ... 17
    Tomato sauce 148
trout
    Deep trout fish cakes with lemon butter
       and chive sauce 31
    Trout and fennel gravlax with
       mustard and horseradish sauce 164
    Whole baked trout with crunchy bacon
       and hyssop stuffing 167

V
venison (see also game)
    Venison and red wine stew with herby dumplings. 176
    Venison burgers with apple balsamic
       and beetroot relish 179

Y
Yogurt 14
Yogurt cheese 14
    Orange yogurt cheese cheesecake 32
Yorkshire puddings 138

Editorial director: Anne Furniss
Project editor: Simon Davis
Art direction & design:
Victoria Sawdon at Big Fish®
Photographer: Andrew Montgomery
Illustrator: Ariel Cortese at Big Fish®
Recipe consultant: Debbie Major
Props stylist: Jo Harris
Production: James Finan, Vincent Smith

First published in 2013 by
Quadrille Publishing Limited
Alhambra House, 27–31
Charing Cross Road,
London WC2H 0LS
www.quadrille.co.uk

Text © 2013 YEO VALLEY

Photography © 2013 Andrew Montgomery

Design and layout © 2013
Quadrille Publishing Limited

Cataloguing in Publication Data:
a catalogue record for this book is
available from the British Library.

UK TRADE: 978 184949 266 9
YEO: 978 184949 302 4

Printed in
The West Country

Thank you

To Dad for giving us so much opportunity.

To Vicky for her patience, her beautiful design and great creativity.
To Perry, Lee and Ariel from Big Fish.
To Andrew for his fantastic photography.
To Debbie for her help with inspirational recipes and cooking.
To Anne and Simon from Quadrille for their experience and huge support.
To Tim and Sarah, Amanda and Phil, Mum and all at Yeo Valley.

Lastly to Clive, Emily, Alice, William and Maisie
for their loving and enthusiastic support.

This book, my first, has been a huge learning curve and a big team effort.
It's been brilliant – a huge thank you to everyone involved!

Come along and say hello!

Whether you fancy paying a visit to our organic gardens and
tea room; you'd like a few tranquil days at our eco retreat
Wills Barn; or you want to learn something new at our
Yeoniversity, we'd love to hear from you. Oh, and we also
have some amazing spaces at our HQ that you can hire for
meetings or events, and we do farm tours, too. You'll find
all the details you need at www.yeovalley.co.uk.